Praise for Ellen and

MW00592808

"Easy and fun to read, this book goes beyond the typical branding exercises and provides unique and insightful tools to communicate your value confidently and authentically. A little gem of a book that can be read again and again as one evolves in their professional and personal journey."

Menexia Tsoubeli, Ph.D., Director R&D, Campbell's Soup Company

"Ellen creatively captured my brand in a way that reflects my style, energy and values. Her extraordinary personal attention was above and beyond what I expected. Ellen's in-depth branding process encouraged me to focus on my strengths and abilities and how I wanted to communicate that as a professional Realtor."

Patti Camras, Realtor, Coldwell Banker

"Creating and sustaining an inclusive environment starts with great leaders who are highly self-aware and who have mastered self-leadership. Ellen's personal branding book is a must read for anyone who wants to distinguish themselves as a world-class leader who inspires diversity, inclusion and innovation."

Stacè Middlebrooks Head of Diversity & Inclusion
Southern California Edison (SCE)

"At last! Professional branding defined! A great story about creating your brand through finding your true and unique self. Ellen's book is an interesting, useful and valuable guide to changing the way you view, acknowledge and leverage your talents."

Amanda Page, Change Lead, Cisco, UK

BRANDED FOR LIFE!

8 Elements to Transform

Your Personal Brand, Career and Life

By: Ellen Looyen
"America's Leader in Personal Branding"

M⊙tivational PRESS®
LEADERS IN GLOBAL PUBLISHING

To Chelsea — A First Class Brand! All Looye, Thank you!

Published by Motivational Press, Inc.
1777 Aurora Road
Melbourne, Florida, 32935
www.MotivationalPress.com

Copyright 2015 © by Ellen Looyen

All Rights Reserved

No part of this book may be reproduced or transmitted in any form by any means: graphic, electronic, or mechanical, including photocopying, recording, taping or by any information storage or retrieval system without permission, in writing, from the authors, except for the inclusion of brief quotations in a review, article, book, or academic paper. The authors and publisher of this book and the associated materials have used their best efforts in preparing this material. The authors and publisher make no representations or warranties with respect to accuracy, applicability, fitness or completeness of the contents of this material. They disclaim any warranties expressed or implied, merchantability, or fitness for any particular purpose. The authors and publisher shall in no event be held liable for any loss or other damages, including but not limited to special, incidental, consequential, or other damages. If you have any questions or concerns, the advice of a competent professional should be sought.

Manufactured in the United States of America.

ISBN: 978-1-62865-179-9

Contents

In loving memory of
Lance Miller,
Renaissance Man, Sailor
and the best friend I've ever had.

Acknowledgments

My deepest gratitude to:

Jaqueline Kyle, my 'taskmaster' and book writing coach, for her professionalism, commitment and brilliance.

Carolyn Pon, and The Professional Businesswomen of California (PBWC.org), for their unwavering support of my work (for over three years and still counting).

My earliest adopters, including: Stacè Middlebrooks, Amanda Page, Leah Whitman, Avis Beiden, Menexia Tsoubeli and countless others in over 60 countries.

My dear friends and cheerleaders: Susan Wingfield and Michelle Burke; and Sarah Tolson, a former client who helped proof read my book.

Sunil Bhaskaran, Executive Business Coach and former client, for his wonderful Foreword.

My parents, Ruby and Fred Frankfort; and other family members, including: my cousins, Robert and Michael and my brother, Gary.

My loyal support staff (for many years), without whom I could not function: Dolores McElroy, my graphics pro and Ken Klages, for his IT and Web brilliance.

My Black Lab, Lily, who, for over ten years, has been there for me through thick and thin...***Dogs Rule!***

Foreword

As someone who has trained and coached thousands of entrepreneurs and business professionals since 1991, I have observed that personal branding produces a very high return on investment—not just monetarily over time, but also in the subjective, but critical, areas of self expression, joy, happiness and professional creativity.

This book represents an outstanding introduction to personal branding. It clearly outlines the process and also demonstrates Ellen's mastery in using story-telling and objective facts to weave a powerful narrative to enable you to present yourself in the most professional (and profitable) way.

My association with Ellen began a few years ago. After several years of searching for a branding professional to help me brand both myself, and my coaching business, I was immediately drawn to Ellen. She was clear and concise in what needed to be produced and how to make it happen.

Ellen demonstrated a Yoda-like ability to glean the best of me, while asking some very straightforward questions. I was not the kind of person to shirk from information that made sense and could help me direct my business, so I decided to hire Ellen (from a group of about 25 contenders).

My branding results were remarkable in the following ways:

1. The marketing materials that resulted from the partnership with Ellen were outstanding and far exceeded my expectations, in terms of messaging, artistry and their overall ability to instantly connect with my perfect clients.

2. The materials have measurably attracted higher quality clients with an eye for not just style, but for content of message, as well.

3. The quality of business opportunities, joint ventures and speaking opportunities has gone up by more than 50% since the branding exercise—consistently, each year, for the past three years!

If you are someone who has experienced disappointing marketing results or branding programs that have not delivered on their promise, this book and Ellen's step-by-step, time-tested process will help you move through any of the obstacles that most of us have experienced.

Additionally, Ellen's focus on energetic presence, emotional intelligence and all of the *inner* workings of a personal brand, will help readers identify the 'blind spots' which may be keeping them from enjoying the likeability and success they desire.

The personal branding process that Ellen has so skillfully demystified in this book is very clear and logical. As she shares the branding stories of her two main characters, Ellen inspires readers to craft compelling stories of the uniqueness and value of their own work contributions, an imperative element to successful personal branding.

I highly recommend going through this book thoroughly, with pen and paper in hand, as Ellen guides you to masterfully articulate the many gifts and talents you have to share with those people you most want to attract and influence.

Sunil Bhaskaran
Executive Business Coach

Introduction

I've always been an original, but it took me a very long time to appreciate my own uniqueness.

As a six-foot tall woman, I knew a lot about standing out in a crowd (literally). In my high school yearbook, the quote under my photo said, "Individuality is the salt of life." At the time, I was very upset by that quote; I wanted to be like everyone else and just fit in!

Years later, standing out from a crowd of look-alikes was what I built my career on. A fortune cookie I received a few years ago best summed it up. The message read: "You discover hidden treasure where others see nothing unusual." As a branding specialist, that is exactly what I do every day. I look for the "golden nuggets" and for what makes people and their businesses uniquely valuable.

You see, it is impossible to succeed, to distinguish yourself, and to be remembered, if you strive to be just another face in the crowd. Successful businesses and business people need to *stand out* from the crowd. They need to be remembered. They need to stand for something. In short, businesses and people alike, both need compelling brands.

You already have a personal brand...whether you know it, or not!

When people hear your name, several things instantly come to mind. But are they the perceptions that you would choose for people to have of you? They should be, because your career might just depend on it. Personal brand management is for everybody...and it's especially for those wanting to move ahead in their profession, climb the corporate ladder or attract new clients.

Personal Branding is about how others perceive and experience your value and the impressions you leave behind. A critical tool for business and career success (like a current resume, a LinkedIn profile or a website), your personal brand should convey the very best version of yourself, communicate your uniqueness and value, and *energetically* connect to those you most want to influence. There's a direct correlation between how well you're able to confidently broadcast your *self-worth* and the value of your work product, with your *net worth* and your ability to rapidly advance your career or grow your business.

You might already have an idea of what a brand is: the logo on your car, a distinctive color scheme for your favorite sports team, a mission statement written on a wall of a business. What most individuals don't realize is that people have brands too; and whether you want one or not, you already have one. So what does your personal brand say about you?

Unlike most personal branding books, this book is really about taking a profound journey into yourself and into your own uniqueness and value as a professional (as well as a human being). This is a book about self-awareness and self-appreciation and about building an authentic personal brand from the inside-out. The brand and influence-building tools in this book take the form of an inquiry into who you are being and how that influences your work. Remember, that it is less about 'what you do' and more about 'who you are *being*' when you do what you do.

The exercises in this book were designed to encourage mindfulness, emotional intelligence and honest self-reflection. When you redefine your personal brand in such a conscious and authentic way, and begin to own the origin and energy of your personal impact and brand on others, it will change the game and put you in a whole new league, while remaining true to yourself.

What's in it FROM me (versus what's in it FOR me)?

If you are like most, you are probably really good at what you do, but feel uncomfortable standing out or bragging about yourself by tooting your own horn. Instead of arrogantly boasting about yourself and your accomplishments, you can give a voice to your contribution of value by positioning yourself as a 'Thought Leader' with many skills and insights to share.

No matter what your situation is, whether you own a business or you're employed by one, you no longer have to be defined by a mere professional title or job description. Starting right now, I encourage you to think of yourself as the CEO of your own personal brand. Your company owns your job, but YOU own your career and your professional brand! No longer will anyone else have control over your career destiny, once you learn to position and package yourself as the unique and valuable person you are.

Origins of This Book

I have always stepped out of the crowd to blaze my own trail. I knew as soon as I arrived at Temple University, that I wanted to major in Philosophy. As a seeker of truth, I was always asking questions and searching for deeper meaning. Majoring in Philosophy, while an unconventional choice, taught me to analyze and distill things down to their essence. Little did I know then, how that choice of a major would later help me in my future work as a branding specialist.

However, I still had to have some real life experiences before I would discover the true power of my *Eight Elements of Influence*. At the beginning of my career, I was one of the first women in Sales at IBM. I was very young and it was at the height of the Women's Movement. I quickly realized that to be taken seriously and be respected, I had to be extra mindful about managing the impressions I left behind.

It turned out that my early career experience as a professional salesperson at IBM (and later at Xerox Corporation), has influenced everything I've been doing since those days. I learned that people only cared about 'what was in it for them' and that whatever I was promoting needed to solve their problems. If I wasn't able to clearly articulate the value and benefits of the products I was selling, I would not close the sale.

This critical insight guided all of my work; especially when, many years later, I became a marketing consultant, specializing in helping small businesses articulate their uniqueness and value. I designed marketing materials for consultants, coaches, lawyers, Realtors, financial planners, and other service professionals. I created stellar presentations to attract more clients to their various services; yet there was sometimes a disconnect from the professional brand and the actual person providing the service.

After studying and interviewing my clients, I discovered that all the promotional brochures and websites in the world could not close business, if the person providing the service did not convey the same level of confidence that their marketing materials portrayed. In other words, there was a lack of congruence between the business brand and the personal brand of the professional trying to sell their services.

Most of my life, people have described me as "charismatic." At first I didn't understand why that was true; but I did notice I was able to easily attract people and opportunities to me. I always wanted to understand this natural gift I was lucky to possess. I began reading everything I could find on the subject of 'Charisma' (that almost mythical 'It Factor' that successful people used to emotionally connect and influence those around them).

As a result of years of research, I created my "Eight Elements of Influence" (which, by the way, spell out the word "Charisma"), to help self-employed entrepreneurs and corporate professionals move their careers forward.

After speaking to groups and teaching the *Eight Elements* to my coaching clients, I realized how many more people were in need of this knowledge. To teach the *Eight Elements* to the masses, I created an eLearning course with lessons and self-paced activities for students to work through, to craft their own personal brand.

Most people are clueless about their personal impact. Therefore, this book begins with readers becoming more aware of how they are impacting the people they most want to influence. It concludes with the integration of my *Eight Elements of Influence* to help readers *become* the personal brand that people instantly like, trust and connect with.

After delivering a one-hour webinar several years ago (with record-breaking attendance), for the Professional Business Women of California (a non-profit, supporting 'emerging' female leaders in Corporate America), they decided to offer my live, 8-week, eLearning webinars to their global community of 30,000. The successful joint venture eLearning programs, were PBWC's most highly attended offerings, drawing people from over 60 countries. The success of this partnership re-energized my career and brought my work to the attention of many Fortune 500 companies like Cisco, HP, Oracle, Visa, eBay and countless other American companies doing business around the world.

In Corporate America, I have helped engineers, financial analysts, sales and marketing departments and research & development professionals, from middle management to top executives. After all these years of helping such a diverse group of both men and women all over the world, I've come to appreciate how my program is really for anyone who wants to get ahead, as it meets people wherever they currently are in their careers.

At first I was very surprised that leading companies would invest in personal brand development for their employees. Later, I learned how important it was for them to be able to attract and retain great employees, especially with all the new, 'sexy' companies competing for top talent (like the Googles and the Facebooks of the world, offering everything from free gourmet food to massages).

The use of 'Story Telling' in this book

One of the most important components to a successful personal brand is being able to tell a story about how you brought value to a client, stakeholder or co-worker.

With this in mind, I have created two avatars for you, the reader, to give you perspective on your own personal branding journey. These characters, Sanjay and Susan, are composite characters, based on the thousands of people I've helped. I want my readers to go through the personal branding experience in much of the same way we viscerally "experience" brands through a deep emotional connection.

As you 'experience' the personal branding process and learn to employ my *Eight Elements of Influence,* you will probably feel the same fear, frustration and ultimate success that many of my clients have experienced going through this process of self-discovery. Hopefully, by keeping up with the adventures of Sanjay and Susan, you will come to see that the doubts and trials you face in your own process are normal and absolutely surmountable.

As Sanjay and Susan go through my branding webinar, I highly encourage you to embrace their experience first-hand and follow along with all of the written exercises. These exercises can be found, in the same order they appear in the story, in the Appendix at the back of this book.

By taking my "Influence Inquiry" before you learn how to integrate the *Eight Elements of Influence,* you will immediately see where *your* work needs to begin.

Benefits

After completing all of the exercises in this book and successfully integrating my *Eight Elements of Influence,* you will have created a compelling personal brand; and you will be perceived as the *influential* expert you really are. As you take an honest inventory of all of your many competencies, you will also be boosting your self-confidence along the way. Your enhanced self-worth will in turn, build your net worth. No longer will your own 'blind spots' and overly reactive emotional triggers hold you back; instead you will become more confident, present and successful. Rather than working so hard to get people to like you and feel comfortable around you, you will become a person who's likeable and comfortable to be around!

You will learn that the secret to effectively managing your personal brand and having greater influence lies in the present moment. You will also discover how your own thinking shapes the way you see and experience life. As Wayne Dyer, the spiritual 'Thought Leader' and best-selling author, so eloquently said: "When you change the way you look at things, the things you look at change." When you are feeling calm, centered, relaxed and truly in the present moment, you'll be broadcasting your most 'energetically attractive' and charismatic self, and your personal brand will be irresistible to the many people you wish to influence!

This book and the exercises in the Appendix will help you:

- Understand the current perceptions people have of you, and improve them
- Articulate your own uniqueness and value
- Redefine and re-tell your own unique professional branding story
- Manage your own state of mind, to proactively manage your career destiny
- Take an honest inventory of your emotional intelligence, including your 'blind spots' and emotional triggers
- Become a more confident and effective communicator, collaborator and team member
- Radiate such an irresistible energetic of presence, confidence, influence and authenticity, that you become the person that people like, hire and promote!

It is my most sincere wish that you take the time-tested lessons in this book and implement them for greater success in every part of your life. Take notes, bring a highlighter and turn the page, to take your career (and your life) to the next level!

Ellen Looyen, *America's Leader in Personal Branding*

Prologue

––––––

S usan's last meeting of the day had run late, and what was worse, they hadn't signed the agreement. As she set the dinner table, Susan ran the meeting through her head one more time.

It should have been a no-brainer.

As a financial planner specializing in women and couples with young families, her presentation to John and Sarah had made sense. They were exactly the kind of clients she looked for. So when Susan had finished her presentation and John said, "They'd think about it and get back to her," she didn't quite know what to do. They should have said 'yes' right away. She had quickly backed up her PowerPoint slides and had gone over the major points of her recommended financial plan one more time. The answer had still been, "We'll think about it." Her mind had been racing so much, that she wasn't sure what had been said after that. She just left. Without the signed financial planning agreement.

The beeping of the oven's digital clock pulled Susan back into the moment. Unfortunately, it was quickly followed by the wail of her three-year-old, finally having enough of her brother's game. Susan sighed and wondered where Sanjay was.

Her husband, Sanjay, usually picked up the kids from daycare after work. As a mid-level engineer at a Fortune 100 Silicon Valley company, his hours were usually pretty regular. In fact, Sanjay was as dependable as the day was long, in every aspect of their lives.

Just then, the garage door started churning. *Ah! He's home,* Susan thought. *Thank goodness!*

Sure enough, Sanjay came through the door a minute later, lugging his laptop bag and juggling his trusty coffee mug with a handful of flyers and handwritten notes. He smiled widely when he saw his family gathered around the table. He seemed to be drinking them in with purposeful affection.

Dumping his belongings in a chair, he swarmed the table, giving her, their son Josh and their daughter Lily each a kiss and a hug in turn. *What is going on?* Susan wondered.

"Was traffic that bad?" she quirked an eyebrow at Sanjay as he settled down into his accustomed chair.

"Nothing like that," Sanjay replied with a smile. "That conference I had to stay late for? It was good. Really insightful. I just want to tell each and every one of you that *what you appreciate, appreciates*[1] and I appreciate each one of you." He finished his statement by gently bopping Lily on the nose, causing her to giggle.

Must have been one heck of a conference, Susan pondered. Sanjay was always very attentive to his family, but never so affectionate. This was an unexpected and welcome change. Susan was curious and wanted to ask more.

It wasn't until much later, when the kids were in bed, if not yet asleep, that Sanjay and Susan finally had time to sit down together. It was their usual custom for Sanjay to sit on the couch and Susan to throw her legs over his lap while they channel surfed together. However, something else was on Sanjay's mind tonight. He was restless and after a few minutes of flipping programs, he turned the TV off.

He turned to her, "I've got to tell you about one of the speakers we had at this conference and some of the things she got me thinking about."

---

[1] *The Soul of Money,* By: Lynne Twist

* * *

The next day found Susan sitting in front of her computer, repeatedly hitting the refresh button on her email. No word yet from John and Sarah. *It's too early,* Susan scolded herself.

When her phone buzzed, Susan leapt to answer, grateful for the distraction.

"Guess what?" said the text from Sanjay.

"What?" she answered.

"My boss really liked the speaker I told you about from the conference yesterday too!" The focus of Sanjay's conference was on personal branding, professional development and leadership training for introverted engineer types who the company had on their leadership fast track.

"By the way, there's an eLearning webinar program coming up later this month. And it's open to the general public. Cubicle dwellers and entrepreneurs. You should join us!"

"I'll think about it," Susan hedged.

Just then, Susan was distracted by the *ding* of her email. A quick toggle to Outlook and Susan's heart skipped a beat. John and Sarah!

Susan quickly scanned the email, feeling her heart sink into her stomach until she felt like she was going to be sick. *"Not interested at this time..."*

She read it again more slowly, this time growing angry. How could they *not* be interested in her? She handled accounts like theirs every day!

Another *ding!* pulled Susan out of her mental rant. This one was an email from the San Francisco Commonwealth Club advertising their upcoming events. Right on top was a personal branding talk happening next week, with Ellen Looyen. Amazed by the coincidence of Ellen, being the same speaker Sanjay was gushing about, presenting at one of Susan's favorite venues for inspiring speakers of all kinds! Stunned by the serendipity of it all, Susan quickly signed up.

Chapter One

———————

Influence and Personal Branding

Susan arrived at the San Francisco Commonwealth Club early, working the room, giving out a few business cards, shaking hands, and giving a wave to a competing financial advisor she knew. As the start time for Ellen's Keynote talk grew closer, Susan claimed a seat in the back, telling herself that she had an easy escape if this turned out to be a waste of time.

The crowd clapped with enthusiasm as Ellen came up on stage. There was definitely something unique about Ellen...she was enthusiastic, energetic, and charming and she seemed to possess a rare combination of warmth, authenticity and strength. Everyone immediately felt her presence, as the room got instantly quiet.

"Thank you everyone for coming here this evening. My name is Ellen Looyen and I have been a branding expert for over two decades. What most people believe is that branding is only for big companies and their products. But branding is really for anyone who wants to get ahead in their life. So, I'm curious, how many of you have a personal brand?"

A few scattered hands raised in the crowd.

"This is actually a trick question! Everyone here already has a personal brand. You have a personal brand, whether you are managing it, or not. Jeff Bezos, the founder of Amazon.com, said *your personal brand is what people are saying about you when you're not in the room*. When people hear your name, several perceptions instantly come to mind. But are they the perceptions you would *choose*? If not, they *should* be, as your career might just depend on it!

———

"This evening's talk is meant to create a more meaningful context for building your personal brand. And by the way, I approach personal branding in a very different way than what you might expect. I see personal branding as an *inside job*. So, it's really less about what you *do* and more about how people experience you as a person, doing what you do so well.

"*Remember, we're not human doings—we're human beings; and personal branding is all about how people experience you...Brands are felt!*"

Susan shifted in her chair. This *was* different. Rapidly she rummaged through her purse until she retrieved a notebook and pen.

"I want to kick off my talk tonight with an important quote that has everything to do with personal branding (and life):

The way you do one thing, is the way you do everything.

"I'll say that again. It's very important. I heard this from a great spiritual teacher of mine, many years ago; and I see it as so true for my life, as well as for my personal brand. *The way you do one thing is the way you do everything.*

"You see, consistency is a big part of your personal brand. Delivering a consistent experience every time is key to having your brand be trusted by others, and particularly by those you most want to influence."

Susan jotted down the quote and underlined consistency beneath it.

"The way I do personal branding includes an emotional intelligence component, too. Whether you work as a solo entrepreneur, or you are part of a team in a corporation, the more self-aware you are, the more whole and emotionally intelligent you are, the better you are as a team member or business owner.

"One of my very first clients, Dr. Green, had been working inside a hospital as a psychotherapist for over thirty years. She had just turned sixty and decided that it was time to pursue her dream of having her own private psychotherapy practice and hanging out her own shingle.

She hired me to brand her new practice, and when I presented her with her new logo, brochure, website and her overall new and improved brand, she started sobbing. Naturally I asked her what was wrong.

Dr. Green stated: "For thirty years as a therapist, it's been my job to really see people, really 'get' them. My role has been to reflect their value back to them, in a way that helps them appreciate their own uniqueness and value. But, I've never had anyone do that for *me*...until just now!

"Let me tell you, it was pretty frightening, having my client crying like that because someone finally 'got' their value in a way they weren't able to articulate before! But I must confess that this same reaction actually happens a lot. We all need someone to acknowledge us and hold a mirror up, so we can see ourselves as others do and gain a new-found appreciation for our own special value.

"For those of you who hate the idea of 'tooting your own horn' or really have a big problem with the whole idea of self-promotion, you might be thinking that you're in the wrong room. That couldn't be further from the truth! It is true, that in many cultures, it's a real no-no to stand out, call attention to yourself, or think you're someone extra-special."

Susan immediately scratched down Sanjay's name, "stand out" and "culture." He never wanted to stand out. Now, she realized that it was probably a cultural thing—Sanjay's modesty and humility, was something she never quite understood about her Indian husband until just now.

On stage, Ellen continued, "This isn't just a frivolous, 'Look at me. Aren't I terrific? I built my personal brand and now I'm so great.' No. It's more about the Return on Investment (ROI), and your unique and valuable contribution to your company's bottom line, or to your clients, if you're in business for yourself. Can you easily and clearly articulate the contribution of value that you bring to your own business, or to the overall corporate brand of your employer?

"Building your personal brand and managing it effectively is not about bragging; but quite the contrary. My branding process will help you understand the Return On Investment that your company or clients receive from paying you for your services. If you're not really clear about that and you're not able to articulate your own value, you may not have your job or your own business forever!

"By the way, it's great job security to have a well-managed personal brand. It's great career security to feel confident and be able to articulate your own value in such a way that people really *get* your special contributions.

"What are the components of a well managed brand? First, you need to have an *emotional connection*. It's one of the hallmarks of branding, in general, whether we're talking about a breakfast cereal brand or an automobile's unique brand. You need to make an emotional connection with the people that you want to interact with your brand. That emotional connection engenders instant likeability, trust and rapport and all the things that are so important to having a successful brand."

Susan jotted down 'Emotional Connection.' After a moment she followed it with a question mark. What was the emotional connection of her brand?

"Another hallmark of a very successful brand," Ellen continued, "is the idea of differentiation. What makes you different? It doesn't matter if you are a person or a product or a service. In a corporation, you bring your own uniqueness to your position. That uniqueness is about you, how you show up and how you're *being* in your job. Not just how you're doing your job, but how you're *being* while you're fulfilling your role. So differentiation, how you separate yourself from every other person is one of the keys to your personal brand's success.

"The next key to success is *positioning*. Positioning aims to occupy a distinct position in the mind of the people you most want to influence. Recently a former client of mine, Pamela, who works for a very large company, came to town on business and we had dinner. Pamela had gone through my personal brand and influence-building coaching program several years ago. What she told me about her experience was so personally rewarding for me.

"Pamela is in R&D, and she shared that the brand and influence-building coaching we did together a couple of years ago, changed the game for her and put her in a whole new league, particularly because of smart positioning. Once she had the words to describe her own uniqueness and position her value and expertise as so intrinsically important to her company's success, it got other people seeing her that way, too. She'd already gotten two promotions since completing our branding work together. Pamela felt like she and her personal brand were very congruent. She was able to articulate her value in a way that was true to herself and came across as very authentic to the people she most wanted to influence.

"The most amazing thing was that she even looked and sounded so different. I asked her if she had any 'work done' as she looked more youthful and vibrant with her new-found confidence and deep belief in her own value! She assured me that it was all an inside job, as she once again expressed her heartfelt gratitude.

Ellen took a moment to pause and smile mischievously. "I'm going to play a little game with you about a company that has done a great job of positioning. Think for a moment about a European car manufacturer who has positioned their brand name to go with the attribute of "safety."

There was some muttering at the front of the room. Ellen held up a finger in forbearance. "Hang on everyone. I know you have something in mind already. On the count of three, everyone say their answer out loud. One. Two. Three."

Immediately the audience responded in unison with, "Volvo!"

"That's right!" Ellen laughed. "Volvo has done such a successful job of aligning and positioning their brand with the attribute of safety. Are they safer than any other car? Maybe. Maybe, not. But they have cleverly

Chapter One

positioned themselves so that most people think of the *Volvo* brand when they think *safety*.

"With this in mind, I'd like you to take a minute right now and jot down what you would like people to think about you when your name is mentioned. What do you want to be known for, known as, or known for knowing? What are 2-3 attributes, that you want people to associate with you and your personal brand?"

Susan stared at the page. The first word she thought of was 'Smart.' Could smart be a good attribute? Or was it just pompous and arrogant? She gritted her teeth and wrote it down.

"As I said earlier, branding is about delivering a consistent experience. If you asked five co-workers or clients what three adjectives they would use to describe you, would any match what is on your paper now? Would their answers match each other? Delivering a consistent experience every time is important, because brands are felt, and they're felt, emotionally, first and foremost.

"So, how do you want to be perceived by those you most want to influence?

Maybe you want to be perceived as a 'Thought Leader' in your field. Starting today, I'd like all of you to think of yourself that way. Wouldn't it be great if your clients, stakeholders or co-workers had so much respect for what you know and can do for them, that you actually become the go-to person for learning more about _____(you can fill in the blank with your expertise). What do you know that makes you so skilled at what you help others do? Please take a moment during the upcoming break to jot down some ideas. It's very important to set the intention of your personal brand right from the get-go."

The audience around Susan got up to stretch, but she didn't notice at first. She was staring at her paper. *How do I want to be perceived by those I most want to influence? And what unique benefits do I have to offer my clients as an expert or 'Thought Leader' in Financial Planning?*

30

* * *

Outside the conference room, small groups were buzzing about Ellen's talk and their own 'light bulb moments.' "Susan!" came a familiar voice from the opposite side of the room. "Over here!"

Susan made her way towards the voice, still wrapped up in her own thoughts and feelings about the first part of the talk. It wasn't until she was right on top of the group, that she realized who had called her name.

"There you are!" gushed Amy, a regular networker and professional friend. Amy quickly snared Susan's arm and pulled her into the circle. "Susan, this is MJ. MJ is a former branding client of Ellen's and she's here from London!"

MJ smiled broadly and laughed. "You make me sound like a minor celebrity!" Her accent was sharp and fast, with the sing-song lilt of the English.

"Did you come just for Ellen's speech?" Susan asked rather incredulously.

"Oh, no!" MJ assured her. "I happened to be in town and I never miss a chance to hear Ellen speak." She paused thoughtfully. "Actually, I am here in the US because of Ellen, but in a different way. I work for a huge American IT company, outside of London, but the headquarters are located here in the Silicon Valley. A couple of months ago, a California executive was visiting and we struck up a conversation in the hall. It was like Ellen had been prepping me for that exact moment, as she helped me build my personal brand just a few months before. I told him my personal brand *story*, subtly highlighting the many benefits and results that I've gotten for my team members and stakeholders...and boom! I'm out here working on a special high-level project, as an expert from my department!"

"Oh, wow!" Amy exclaimed. "That is so amazing. I wish I could travel on the company's dime!"

"You and everyone else," Susan agreed. After a few more minutes of chitchat, Susan excused herself to go find a seat closer to the stage. It wasn't too long before Ellen returned and launched into the second half of her talk.

"For all the corporate professionals here tonight, I want you to remember that you're the CEO of your own brand; and starting today I'd like you to approach your career much more entrepreneurially. That's going to serve you well, especially as you change companies and careers. Some of you will not be at your job for the rest of your life, working for the same company, or even in the same profession. Some of you will move on to other careers, but you'll always take your personal brand and all of your accomplishments with you. Learning how to manage your brand now, is going to be something that's going to serve you well as you further your career, whether you stay with the same company, or you move on."

"Reid Hoffman, Founder of the leading professional networking site, LinkedIn, said in a Newsweek quote many years ago, 'Young people need to think about their careers more like a business, and to think about their brand. They need to learn how to differentiate themselves, and have business intelligence to be the entrepreneurs of their own lives.'

Susan agreed with that whole-heartedly. She and Sanjay had met at work. But shortly after their wedding, she had thrown in the towel, deciding she wanted to work for herself; and she dedicated herself to building her financial advisor career. Some of her earliest clients were people who trusted her from the work and the personal brand she had developed in her first career (way before she even knew she had a brand!).

"It's so exciting to me that multi-national companies are finally investing in personal brand development for their employees. In order to attract and retain top talent, many major corporations are now helping their employees build their professional brands, so that they have a more engaged workforce. In other words, they don't want employees to stay at a company when they're just hanging out for the paycheck. Frankly, I really don't understand how you can go to the same job everyday without feeling engaged, useful, and valued for your expertise.

"The basic thing I want to say here is this: *Your company owns your job, but you own your career.*"

Susan wrote 'I own my career' on her notepad and then underlined it twice. Just writing it made her feel empowered and ready to take charge of her personal brand!

"Now we are going to change gears for a minute. We talked about what branding is. Now we are going to delve a bit deeper and talk about *The Three Sources of Power.*[2] What if you had the power to effortlessly influence people into making decisions in your favor? What if you could close more sales, get greater buy-in for your ideas and get promoted more often? Be honest, wouldn't you love to capture the imagination of the people you most want to influence?

The power of influence is the way to do this. But influence is just one of three different sources of power. The first source of power is formal authority. We understand this one pretty well. It's associated with a leader's position or their job title. In Corporate America, we have Manager, Director, Senior Director, VP, Executive VP, etc. All different titles up and down the line (and each one stands for a different level of power).

"You get your authority by virtue of your title. I think that's clearly understood.

"The second form of power is persuasion. And that's the application of logic and evidence to influence others. The ability to persuade is a good skill to have. But it's more about strategy and how 'if I do this, then people might do that.' It's very logical and usually requires some evidence, research and facts to influence others.

"The third form of power is the one that excites me the most. It is

---

[2]   From: "Leadership Essentials" SkillSoft

the power of influence. Influence is the ability to effect change without exerting any authority, whatsoever. You effect change by virtue of who you are and how you show up. Your influence naturally exudes out of you, and instantly and effortlessly, inspires other people around you to entrust projects, promotions, purchases, and confidence in you."

Huh, Susan thought. *I wish I knew all of this before I met with John and Sarah the other night. Because now I can see how 'strategic' I was being, overusing the art of persuasion to convince John to hire me (and I didn't even do that very well)!*

"I want you to really focus on the concept of influence as being critical to a successful personal brand. So now that leads me to the subject of your overall energetic presence; and I want to talk about those hidden qualities that make us so *energetically* influential.

"*Leaders and Influencers are people who are able to express strength and warmth simultaneously.* According to the book "Compelling People,"[3] the Harvard research on the two hidden qualities that are most influential, strength is defined as a person's capacity to make things happen with abilities and force of will. When people project strength, they command our respect.

"But strength alone isn't enough! Researchers have found that what makes people most compelling is their ability to be both strong *and* warm. Warmth is such an overlooked and undervalued capability. A lot of people think being warm is being too weak or too feminine. But some of the most powerful and successful male leaders have demonstrated their equal parts of strength and warmth; John F. Kennedy and Nelson Mandela come to my mind when I think about that rare combination of strength and warmth existing simultaneously!

"I know we all understand the power of strength, but warmth is something very often misunderstood and overlooked. People like strong people who possess lots of warmth, too. It gives people the sense that a

---

[3]   By: John Neffinger and Matthew Kohut

person shares our feelings, interests, and views of the world. So, we like and support warm people.

"I have talked about the three sources of power and I have talked a little about the power to influence, deriving from that rare alchemy of strength and warmth. Now I'm going to dig more into warmth to show you how strength and influence can be derived from it. You see, warm people feel much more authentic to us, they feel more present, and they feel extra-human.

"We've all experienced that feeling of a person's energetic presence. We've all been stuck in meetings with someone who is so negative; and we jokingly call them, "Debbie Downer" because they're bringing down the whole room with their negativity. We've also seen energy that's so positive that it lifts up an entire room.

"That is what your energetic presence is. It's a very 'contagious' energy that is strongly felt by others. If you want to be a leader in your career and in your life, having an 'attractive' and emotionally connecting energetic presence is a vital component to your personal brand.

"We've all heard the word "charismatic" used to define an energetic presence that effortlessly exudes strength and warmth...that intangible 'It Factor' energy that's one of the most powerful forms of persuasion and influence. So how do you get charisma?

"Think for a moment about Oprah. She's an excellent example of a charismatic influencer who's captured the imagination of women throughout the world. She does this by being extra-human versus super-human. I work with a lot of high potential female leaders. And a lot of them are more of the super-human types. They do a million different things. And they think they're being super-human at every one of them. But are they being extra-human?

"We love leaders who are extra-human."

Susan made a note, 'Super-human versus extra-human. Be extra-human!'

"If your brand is known as a very warm brand that people can relate to on an emotional level, you'll be way more successful. If, by your own authenticity and energetic presence you inspire others to be more real and more vulnerable, you will experience much more success.

"Max Weber, a German sociologist at the turn of the last century, called charisma the third form of authority, after law and tradition. Now that's major! In teaching something as intangible as 'charismatic influence', I have deconstructed it down to *Eight Elements,* and they all roll up to you becoming stronger and warmer, and thus, much more influential. The "Eight Elements of Influence" are: 1.) Consciously Manage Your State of Mind 2.) Have Self-Awareness 3.) Artfully Communicate 4.) Radiate Likeability and Empathy 5.) Inspire Confidence 6.) Serve as a Leader 7.) Maintain Presence 8.) Authentically Project Your True Self.

"Now unfortunately, we won't have a chance to dig into each of these *Eight Elements of Influence* tonight. But with that said, I do have a comprehensive eLearning program that will take you through each element and each individual step towards building an influential personal brand. There's more information available in the back of the room.

"For now, I'm going to leave you with a few more thoughts. The first, is that you already have a personal brand and you have ultimate control of it. If you're sitting here feeling like you're running in place and feeling stuck in your career, or thinking, I don't know what my brand is, or what makes me uniquely valuable, you should definitely invest the time and energy into finding out. It can be a career and life-changing process for you, as it has been for so many of my clients!

"The second thing I want to impress upon you, is that you are the only *you* in the world. Many people feel like they are a dime a dozen. Let me assure you, you are the only one that does what you do the way that you do it. You are not a robot; you are not a cog in the machine. You are a human being and who you are *being* on the job is very important.

"The final thing I want to reiterate is that there is no substitute for authenticity and warmth. Whoever you are, whatever you do, you will see an abundance of success in all of your endeavors if you are true to yourself and warm, kind and authentic towards others.

"With that, I'm going to wish you all great success. Thank you so much for *being* here with me tonight."

As the applause died, Susan reviewed her notes. Uplifting words and phrases like 'extra human' and 'I own my career' stared back at her from the page. Alongside them were questions like 'how do I want to be perceived?' Snapping her notebook closed, Susan marched to the back of the room, determined to meet Ellen in-person and continue a personal brand inquiry with her.

Chapter Two

———

Element #1: Consciously Manage Your State of Mind

Susan stared at the screen, wishing the answer would just present itself. After getting so energized from Ellen's talk, she immediately signed up for the personal brand and influence-building eLearning webinar, only to hit a roadblock in the first of many tasks

The Personal Impact Survey, she had learned, was the way to discover how her personal brand was already being perceived by the people she most wanted to influence. It was a series of six simple questions that was supposed to be sent (with a cover letter) to a cross section of five people who have directly experienced working with her professionally. It could be clients, stakeholders, co-workers, colleagues and bosses; but as an independent financial advisor, her colleagues barely knew her name and her co-workers were the other financial advisors that gossiped at the water cooler.

That left her clients.

The list of clients currently displayed on her computer looked like a selection of bombs that may detonate when handled unnecessarily. Not that they hated her. She would know if they did. But what if asking them these six questions made them realize that they didn't like her or didn't want to continue working with her? What if they said really horrible things?

So far, Susan had managed to highlight four clients that she thought would say something nice. Or at least not be downright nasty. She considered sending the fifth one to a client who would likely be too busy to respond.

"Did you hear the news?" Greg, a fellow financial advisor popped into her office.

Susan smiled; she could always count on Greg for the office news. She had never known a gossip quite as enthusiastic as Greg. She didn't even need to wander down to the water cooler!

"Ah... the market crashed and we are all going to die," she joked.

"This is serious!"

Susan arranged her face into a more appropriate and serious face and gestured for Greg to come in and sit.

"Carl was fired this morning!"

"No!" Susan was aghast. "Was he doing something unethical?" Carl had been with the company ten years. She couldn't imagine what he could have done to be terminated.

"Rumor has it, he didn't meet his sales quotas for the last three quarters. Management had enough."

"You're kidding!" Financial advising was a tough career to get into, but most wash outs from poor sales happened in the first three years. For someone with ten years of production under his belt, it was almost unheard of.

"Well they raised those quotas at the beginning of the year, remember? I'm doing okay, but Carl was really struggling to make his numbers."

Oh crap! Susan thought. She remembered the increase in sales quotas at the first of the year, but she had landed two new clients almost immediately and never thought twice about the quota again. How *was* she doing?

She made some more small talk with Greg and then sent him on his way. As soon as he was gone, Susan frantically dug out the dusty manual from the annual kick off meeting. Her heart was pounding.

A quick scan of the compensation and expectation section gave her the answer. She was hitting her numbers. But just barely. Her commissions were good, but assets under management were dangerously close to the line. A look at the hurdles for the next year of production made a pit in her stomach. Susan would need to land a lot of business in the next few months if she wanted to keep her job!

How did this happen? She wondered. Susan had always exceeded her goals by a large margin.

* * *

"Why is this such a big deal?" Sanjay asked.

Susan already regretted trying to talk to Sanjay about the personal branding survey.

When she didn't respond, Sanjay continued, "They already think what they think, right?"

"But what if by asking them, they realize that they *don't like me?* I won't have any clients left!"

"Honey, people think what they think already. Asking them will only help you. What you don't know *can* hurt you."

"So have you sent your surveys out yet?" she knew it was unfair, but she needed to find a chink in his armor. Sometimes it was unbearable how coldly logical he could be.

"Of course. I sent mine out right away."

"Who did you ask?"

"My team, my boss, his boss," Sanjay shrugged.

Susan felt her jaw hanging open and closed it. "Just like that?"

"Why not? They are the people who work with me most. They know how much I contribute. It's not a big deal."

She could tell that he was completely missing the point. Sometimes she wished she could be as dispassionate as he was.

"You're under-performing, right?"

Susan cringed. *Why did she tell him that? Why had she assumed he would be supportive?*

"How are you supposed to complete this personal branding program, and make millions of dollars if you don't do it?" His eyes twinkled at his own joke.

Susan sighed in defeat. "What if they don't like parts about me that I can't change?"

For the first time all night, Sanjay seemed to get that she needed his support. He took her in his arms and kissed the top of her head. "You are an amazing, smart and capable woman. You can do this."

* * *

Sanjay sat in an uncomfortable conference room that had two more people than spaces available at the table. Having come late, he had dragged a chair to the wall and propped his notepad on his knee, preparing to take notes with the rest of his team. On the table was the phone, already dialed into the first of the personal branding global webinar sessions.

"Good Morning," Ellen's voice welcomed them.

"We are going to cover a lot of ground here today. I'm going to start with your Personal Impact Surveys, have a quick Q&A and then I'll be launching into the first of my *Eight Elements of Influence*: "Consciously Manage Your State of Mind."

"So let me start with the statement: You can't change how you are being perceived until you know how people actually see you. And by the way, it's not just about how you perform at your job, as most of us have some gauge of success or failure there. You need to know how you're being perceived as the *person* doing your job.

"Individual perceptions influence the way we respond to each other, and they also influence our perceived value in different situations. The first step towards building your personal brand is to ask for more specific feedback from people who know you in a professional setting—people who have worked with you. And don't be surprised if what others value the most about you is not what you expected! Your Personal Impact Survey (found in the Appendix in the back of this book), will help you see whether the way others see you aligns with how you want to be perceived. The feedback will help give you insight about areas you may need to improve. It also has the extra bonus of collecting useful information and actual sound bites to later quote, to help you articulate your value."

Sound bites? Sanjay didn't like the sound of that. He had been fine with telling Susan to send out her surveys, and he hadn't hesitated to send out his own; but for the first time, he wondered what his colleagues might say about him. And whether it would even be worth quoting as a so-called *sound bite*. He couldn't imagine talking or bragging about himself, never mind using someone else's words to do it!

"Your first big assignment is to identify five people in your network and send them a Personal Impact Survey," Ellen continued. "People who have had the experience of working with you can give you fresh new insights into your own *perceived* value. For best results, choose five or more people you have actually worked with, and who will be willing and able to articulate your work contributions and your unique value.

"Candid feedback is necessary for building a credible and compelling brand. Make sure you also include someone who was relatively easy to work with, and someone who was challenging to work with, too. It's good to send them out to people that you might have had a negative experience with. I have had many clients report back to me, that in sending them out to someone who had a negative experience, it transformed everything. Those people really respected the fact that my clients wanted feedback, even though it might be negative. You might find that this new dialogue reinstates and rejuvenates an old relationship that has gone south.

"Ah, ha! Right on time. A question was just messaged over to me. It's one that comes in fairly frequently. The message reads, 'the Personal Impact Survey questions can be uncomfortable—especially for those from whom we want constructive feedback. What are your suggestions for encouraging objective feedback by possibly making their feedback anonymous?'"

Did Susan ask that? Sanjay was still baffled that Susan would be concerned that her clients wouldn't like her. If they didn't like her, they would take their money elsewhere. Sometimes she just needed to have more faith in herself. He hoped that she was listening to the webinar in her office, too.

Ellen paused thoughtfully. "I don't recommend making it anonymous, because it's really important to see the context of who's saying what. There might be someone who responds with something negative, but you might have had issues with them at work. I think when they're anonymous, it's just not as meaningful.

"I will tell you that people are usually very candid when answering that question. And I've always been surprised by that. I've been using the same methodology for over two decades and the results are proven. People come out the other end with fabulous personal brand success stories. But to get there, sometimes you are going to feel uncomfortable, maybe even vulnerable. And we all want to resist those feelings, especially in the workplace, that's just human nature. We all do that. So give yourself permission to be okay with feedback, to not take it personally and to learn from it, because there's always a kernel of truth in the feedback."

I hope Susan is taking notes.

"Now I'm going to open up the line for a moment to see if there are any other questions before we launch into the meat of today's session. Who has a question that they would like to share?"

An uncomfortable silence drew out before Sanjay's co-worker, David, leaned forward to speak into the phone on the conference table. "Thanks for this Ellen," David started. "I had a question about the number of surveys. I sent out my five when I got the eLearning program, but I have only received one back so far. Should I send out more?"

"Good question!" Ellen replied. "Five is a minimum. It sounds like you didn't send yours out all too long ago, so you might have more coming back to you. If you have the extra time and the desire, send out ten. The more you send out, the greater perspective you will get and the more you will learn."

When no more questions were asked, Ellen launched into the next part of her training. "So far on this call we have dealt with the rational side of your brand. We are digging deeply into how you are *currently* being perceived. Then we will identify how you would *like* to be seen by your peers, bosses, clients and prospects. The gap between these two positions is where we are going to start filling in your own unique personal brand. To do this, we are going to now dive into the emotional side of your brand.

"Before I started working with corporate professionals, I worked mainly with entrepreneurial people like myself. I worked with coaches, consultants, doctors, lawyers, CPAs, financial planners and Realtors. Basically, I crafted brands for professionals of all kinds who had their own service businesses. The service that they personally provided became one and the same as their business brand, because they *were* their business.

"I noticed that I would create beautiful marketing materials for them, but sometimes the entrepreneur felt uncomfortable distributing them. One day, a client came to me and said, 'Ellen, I think you see me a lot better than I see myself.' She said, 'When I market myself with the beautiful materials you developed with me, I feel like I'm marketing someone else, and not me. I don't have the confidence, expertise and self-esteem that your marketing materials imply I do.'

"I went back to past clients and found most of them felt confident about what they did, and the service they provided, *but there was a disconnect about themselves internally, so their inner level of confidence wasn't in alignment.*

"It came down to them feeling like they had an *incongruent personal brand.* What was visible on the outside, in terms of the external brand design and messaging were fabulous and attracted people who wanted to work with them. However, how these professionals 'showed up' in person was a very different story. Prospective clients often got turned off, because nobody wants to work with someone who isn't feeling positive and self-assured and who doesn't show up in a way that is inviting and attractive."

Sanjay quickly wrote down "Incongruence" and then "Susan" next to it.

"That's what prompted me to develop my *Eight Elements of Influence.* I developed these *Eight Elements* and started teaching them to the clients whom I had branded. Oh my goodness! People doubled and tripled their businesses! It was like my *Eight Elements* were casting a magic spell over them!

"The *Eight Elements,* as you will see, work together to create your energetic influence. Your personal brand is not about creating a shiny, but false, image of yourself, the way Madison Avenue ad agencies so often do to market various services and products. It's about bringing out the best version of who you really are.

"Each of the *Eight Elements* inter-relate. They work together as an interwoven web of inner attributes that make up your personal brand. As you learn to incorporate all of the *Eight Elements,* you will naturally enhance your confidence, presence, and influence.

"We are going to be learning, in-depth, over the next eight weeks, all about the *Eight Elements of Influence* and how they all work in concert to create an irresistible energetic presence. If you haven't noticed by now, the first letter of each of these Elements, when combined, spell out the word *Charisma*, making my secret formula for an influential personal brand easy to remember! So everyone, get settled in, and we are going to start with the first of the Elements, Consciously Manage Your State of Mind."

I can handle the idea of incorporating more elements of strength and warmth into my professional brand, but I'm not sure if having charisma is something I'm capable of, Sanjay wondered.

"Did you know that you *energetically* broadcast how you are feeling within seven seconds of entering a room?[4] An important key to managing your personal brand is to manage the "impact" you have on people. Therefore, the first element of the *Eight Elements of Influence* instructs you to become conscious of your all-around energetic presence by maintaining a positive and attractive state of mind.

"Your state of mind is a critical tool for success in both business and life, as your thoughts and feelings influence everything! When you manage your state of mind, to project positive thoughts and exude positive energy in the moment, your calm confidence will naturally attract people to you, and make them want to work with you. Your state of mind projects your belief in your own value and in your own unique abilities.

"Your state of mind is really nothing more than "where you're at" in your head—your internal psychological environment or your inner climate. And it is instantly felt by others. By the way, *insecurity* is also a state of mind that is easily felt and can negatively influence any business interaction. Managing your thinking is one of the most powerful tools used by successful business people.

"Andrew Carnegie, one of the famous early 20th Century industrialists once admitted that the most important key to his success and the most difficult skill for him to develop was the ability to control his own thinking.

---

[4] Albert Mehrabian

"I'm curious...How do you wake up in the morning? What's your first thought upon awakening? Is it, 'I didn't get enough sleep?' Or, rather than waking up reactively, do you state a clear intention for yourself at the beginning of the day?

"I'd like you to do something, as an experiment...Tomorrow, the minute you awaken into consciousness...I want you to see what your first conscious thought is and to notice it. And also notice that you can change it.

"My first awakening thought always used to be, 'Did I get enough sleep?' It was always about that. Now my first thought is, 'Today is going to be a great day.' And I will tell you that by having that intention as my first thought of the day, my day usually turns out much better!

Hmmm. Might be worth a try, Sanjay mused. *If it works, maybe I can train the kids when they're older.*

"Of all of your sources of influence, your state of mind is the one instantly *felt* by others; and it affects all other sources of influence. Your thoughts are directly linked to your moods and to the problems and stresses in your life. Since your own thinking causes your feelings, your feelings become a barometer of how your thoughts are being utilized. Thoughts and feelings are expressed outwardly in words, tone, and non-verbal cues. Becoming aware of your innermost thoughts is the first way to turn around any negative thinking or insecurity. By focusing your thinking on more positive experiences, you will become more attractive to others.

"Peace of mind and happiness are often just one thought away. Your feelings allow you to know the quality of your state of mind in the moment; and the secret to managing your state of mind lies in the present moment. When you are aware of your thoughts in the present moment, you have the power to shift your negative thinking towards more positive thoughts that create better feelings for you.

"We really aren't "victims of circumstance," but rather we are "victims" of our own thinking! When you function more consciously and embrace and maintain present moment awareness, which we will cover more in Element Seven, you are much less likely to mindlessly react to circumstances. Confidence and insecurity are really just states of mind that can both change in an instant!"

Ellen continued on, "Your own thinking shapes the way you see and experience life; and your personal reality is actually molded by your own thinking and state of mind. Therefore, your happiness depends much less on circumstances and much more on your own thoughts and reactions, from moment-to-moment.

"When you are calm, centered, relaxed and truly living in the moment, you have the most "attractive" state of mind. People feel your state of mind and it influences how they feel about working with you.

"Maya Angelou, the late legendary poet, once said, 'People will forget what you said and they will forget what you did; but they will never forget how you made them feel.' When you are fully present with people and able to express a total belief in your own value and abilities, people will experience you as more confident and much more comfortable to be around. When you are calm, people will open up and share more of themselves because of how comfortable your state of mind makes them feel."

Sanjay had a sudden vision of himself, one that he almost immediately dismissed. *He was standing in the center of a crowd and all the people around him were smiling. And he was smiling. He was totally comfortable in a crowd.* Introverted Sanjay suddenly wanted that feeling of contentment and self-acceptance very badly.

"External signals reveal how you feel about yourself and influence how others respond to you. What we deeply feel about ourselves broadcasts externally to the world on a very subtle, yet very persuasive level. A whopping 55% of our influence comes from our body language. Your potential clients, employers and all the people you want to influence, are constantly making emotional decisions about you, simply by the way you make them feel.

"You are being congruent when all of the following are in sync:

- Your words

- Your actions

- The way you make others feel

- Your overall energetic presence

We feel your state of mind the minute we meet you. You may think you're hiding it from us, but you're really not.

"Emotional connection is the most critical element for a successful personal brand; and in order to emotionally connect, your prospects need to feel certain that what you're telling them is true. Saying one thing and feeling another is the quickest way to diminish your influence and destroy a prospect's confidence in your personal brand. Congruence simply means that what you say verbally and non-verbally match; and you are being your true self.

"Saying one thing and feeling another is incongruent; and people will always feel distrustful of you when you are being that way. When you are acting congruent, it puts people at ease and causes them to open up. They feel like they already know you and can easily trust you. "

Well, at least I'm trustworthy, Sanjay thought. *I'm a complete open book. I couldn't fake a smile if I tried.*

"Keep in mind, if someone is meeting you for the first time, that's all they have to go on. Remember that no matter what you think you're hiding from us, you are, in fact, always energetically broadcasting your state of mind. So if you had an issue at home before you left for work, or a bad commute, or whatever the situation was, you are displaying that negativity when you show up.

"We all have bad days. We're all human. Instead of hiding our internal state of mind, just come out with it. Be more honest with people, and tell them you're having a bad day. People really appreciate authenticity."

As Ellen wrapped up the session, encouraged them to send out their five or more surveys (if they hadn't already) and offered to answer more questions via email, Sanjay sat in a stunned silence. He had taken almost no notes, but that idea of him smiling comfortably in a crowd...He couldn't describe the feeling and how badly he wanted it. Suddenly he felt like he was on the right track. Like that could be his. He just needed to put in the work. When he got back to his desk, he sent out three more surveys, just for good measure.

Chapter Three

Element #2: Have Self-Awareness

"So what do you think?" David asked as he plopped down in the break room chair next to Sanjay.

"About?"

"The webinar? What do you think about this personal branding stuff?" David unwrapped a homemade sandwich and took a bite, watching Sanjay while he chewed.

"It's interesting," Sanjay replied neutrally. In truth, he had thought of almost nothing else since the session ended. After sending out an additional three surveys, he had just sat at his desk and stared off into space for a while, lost in memories and ideas for the future. But he wasn't going to tell David that.

"I think this manage your state of mind thing has merit. I talked to Marty about it too." Marty was their boss. Suddenly Sanjay was more interested in where this conversation was going.

"Marty reckons that I need to stop asking so many questions. I never realized I asked so many, but I guess I do. He says it undermines my credibility. Do you think that's true?"

"Yes."

"Oh."

David looked a little hurt, like he might have expected Sanjay to respond differently. But Sanjay always told the truth. In fact, Sanjay planned to make his straightforward and candid personality part of his newly managed personal brand.

David finished his sandwich and left the break room mumbling something about a deadline. Just then, Sanjay's phone buzzed.

"I think I'm lacking congruence." Susan announced without preamble.

"You've always looked very shapely to me." Sanjay teased.

"Stop being a guy. I'm serious," Susan scolded. "I think that I'm undermining the success of my recent appointments. I think that I am outwardly confident and inwardly convinced I'm going to screw it up. And they *know.*"

"Are you sure? Yesterday you were convinced that all your clients hated you. Don't you think you are maybe taking this stuff a little too seriously?"

There was silence on the line. It went on for too long.

"Honey, are you there?"

Susan sighed on the other side of the line. "I really wish I could talk to you."

"You *can* talk to me. We are talking right now."

"About this stuff. About concerns and realizations and feeling like I might learn something about myself."

"I'm sorry. I'm listening. I appreciate you." In truth, the appreciate line had worked so well at dinner the other night that he hoped throwing it in now would save him.

"I appreciate you too," Susan said sadly. "I'll see you at home."

* * *

Sanjay was still pondering his conversation with Susan when he got back to his desk. A quick look at his Inbox got Sanjay excited. The first of his surveys had been returned!

His elation was short lived. As Sanjay read through the responses, he felt a pit growing in his stomach.

1.) How did you come to work with Sanjay?

Sanjay was on the team I inherited from the last project manager.

2.) What is your overall impression of Sanjay and his work?

Sanjay has excellent business acumen and rapidly drives issues to resolution. He has a very unique combination of business and technical proficiency. He is very process focused and supports new initiatives. However, his focus on process in no way compromises his passion for positive results.

3.) What were the major benefits you received from working with Sanjay?

Sanjay will try his very best to deliver what is asked. He has a positive attitude about getting the job done.

4.) How could Sanjay have improved his work product and your experience of working with him?

Overall communication could be improved. In particular, better assessment of a given situation and being more sensitive to the environment to tailor his response, and not be so reactive.

5.) How would you describe your experience with Sanjay to someone else in need of these services?

Sanjay and I have very different styles, which I appreciate. I think he and the team would benefit from him improving his active listening skills. I appreciate his energy and commitment to meeting the high expectations that the team sets for his performance.

6.) What three adjectives would you use to describe Sanjay?

Dependable, Focused, Driven

Sanjay reread his project leader's feedback again. *He doesn't want me on his team!* Yeah, there was a good bit about getting his job done, but

Marty obviously thought about him like he was an inherited piece of machinery. Active listening skills? What did he mean by that?

For the first time in a long time, Sanjay didn't know what to do. Should he confront Marty? What would he even say? What would the repercussions be?

Suddenly Sanjay understood what Susan had been worried about. His stomach churned and he wondered if *anyone* liked him at the office. David did, sure, because he talked to him, but what about everyone else?

He considered calling Susan to get her opinion, but he didn't think she would be receptive. She was pretty annoyed with him on that last phone call. He would have to get to the bottom of this, and *fix this*, himself.

* * *

Susan sat at her desk waiting for the conference call to start. The last one had made her re-think her approach to prospects and how she handled herself. Since then, she had done some reading ahead in the eLearning program and stumbled across the *Ten Tips for Connecting Emotionally* and now she was repeating them to herself before bed, upon waking and before every client meeting (find the *Ten Tips for Connecting Emotionally* in the Appendix).

Even though she was feeling stronger and more confident, she and Sanjay still hadn't patched up their fight from the previous week. If it was a fight at all. She just knew he still wouldn't open up to her, and would shoot down any attempt for her to open up to him. Susan knew it was a long shot, but she was looking forward to this next call—maybe the answer for her and Sanjay's relationship would be on the webinar agenda, too.

Right on time, the hold music stopped and Ellen welcomed them all to their second session. "We're going to start this call with some questions and reactions to last week's session, and see if anyone wants to volunteer the outcome of their Personal Impact Surveys. Then, we are going to jump into Element Two: Have Self-Awareness. We have a lot to cover today, so let's get going!

"Who on the call has a question or observation about last week's session?"

"Yes," a woman's voice chimed through the phone. "I'm calling from Philadelphia; and I have a question about Element One. I work mostly virtually, so I don't understand how my body language or my overall energy determine my first impression."

"That's a fantastic question!" Ellen replied. "Many of us, including myself, do a lot of our work virtually. In that case, your tone of voice becomes vitally important. In the absence of observing a physical presence, *38% of your first impression is based on your tone of voice.*[5] If this is your situation, I suggest you keep a mirror on your desk. I do. Sometimes I can get very intense, and I wear myself out with my own intensity, especially on an important sales call. With a mirror on your desk, you can look at yourself and be reminded to smile and lighten up. And just the act of smiling at yourself, changes your voice tonality and keeps you from inadvertently lowering your energy level. Does that help?"

"Yes, absolutely, Ellen! Thank you for the clarification."

My advice is that the less you are thinking strategically, and the more sensitive you are in understanding your impact on others, the more successful you will be when it comes to influencing others.

When there were no more questions or comments on the previous week, Ellen opened up the floor to results and observations about the Personal Impact Surveys. Susan was relieved and a little envious when someone else jumped in right away. Not that Susan had any intention of sharing; she just couldn't believe that someone was willing to disclose what people had said about them!

---

[5] Albert Mehrabian

"Hi. I'm Maria. I work for Cisco Systems as a Sales Consultant and I'm calling in from Spain."

"Wonderful. Thank you for volunteering!"

"I liked the fourth question, regarding improvement of our work. I liked the idea of learning how I can be better at my work from it. So, I sent it out to my director, my manager, and to a client; and the feedback has been hard to digest, but at least I feel like now I really 'get' where I need to improve."

"Oh, that's wonderful," Ellen replied. "I'm so glad you're also paying attention to the question about how you can improve your services. So many of us cringe at the idea of getting what we perceive as negative feedback. But it's really not negative feedback. You are absolutely right, it is great place to learn where you can improve. Thank you for being on the call and sharing with us so candidly."

"Thank you very much."

Susan glanced at the Personal Impact Surveys she had received so far. Maybe 'easily flustered by questions' and 'sometimes doesn't take our concerns seriously' could be a re-branding starting point. Valuable feedback, but it stung. She wrote down 'not negative' and 'improvement point' in the margin of the survey.

"Let's make the jump now into new content," Ellen continued. "Personal brand-building is about consciously creating the perceptions you want others to have of you. We started this process by asking our co-workers and clients about their experiences working with us. We also need to spend some time defining how we *want* to be perceived. By knowing both where you are now—from your Personal Impact Surveys—and where you want to go—from the exercise we are going to do in a moment, you can start to create a roadmap and an action plan for creating real change.

"It's very important to set the intention of your personal brand right from the get-go. And branding is really about thinking backwards. It's about thinking, 'How do I want to be perceived?' Once you have that fixed in your mind, you can think backwards and find ways to genuinely create those perceptions.

"To help you define what you want your personal brand and perceptions to be, I have three questions for you. These are listed in the eLearning program, but we are going to go over them now. The first is: What makes me and my work unique? Remember, you are not a human *doing*, you are a human *being*. This question refers to who you are 'being' when you work, as much as it refers to your work product, itself.

"The second question is: How do I want to be perceived by others? You may have some ideas of how people have perceived you from the Personal Impact Surveys, but that is in the past. That was your unmanaged brand. This question relates to building your brand for the future. So what attributes do you want people to associate with your name and your work?

"The third question is: Why should people want to work with me? This one really gets to the heart of the matter. What does your existing or future brand offer that will entice people to want to work with you?"

Susan had thought about this a lot since she had been at Ellen's talk at the San Francisco Commonwealth Club. She had written 'smart' then, but now she wrote down 'professional, intelligent, and an expert at financial planning for young families.'

"Yes Ellen, I have a question," a deep baritone voice interrupted. "I've been excited about this personal branding thing, so I've been reading ahead in the eLearning program. In regards to this first Self-Inquiry template question, I'm really struggling for an answer. What if anybody could do my job?"

"You know, my advice to you would be to dig deeper," you could hear Ellen smile as she spoke. "Clients often say that question number one of the Self-Inquiry Survey is the hardest. I have heard people describe themselves as 'a dime a dozen' or 'one more cubicle dweller' or 'just another cog in the machine.' These descriptions are *categorically untrue.* There is something unique that you bring to the office and to your work. Commit to putting in the thought and dig deeper until you find it!"

"Will do! Thanks, Ellen."

"So with a commitment from each of you to spend some time creating your ideal personal brand perceptions, we are going to move into the focus of this call, which is about Element Two: Have Self-Awareness.

"Listen up if you've ever been told something like 'we love the end product of your work; however, sometimes you're too hard to work with; you're pretty moody, or sometimes your emotional well-being isn't in alignment with your work.' There are a lot of people who are very competent at doing what they do, yet they're so difficult for their co-workers, clients and colleagues to work with, that their emotional competencies (or lack thereof) become a glaring deficit.

"Element Two is all about *having self-awareness* and recognizing how your feelings effect your performance. Our emotional feelings will always effect our performance if we don't have self-awareness and self-control around them.

"A by-product of integrating these *Eight Elements* into your personal brand, is that you're going to wind up being not only a much better co-worker or consultant, but a better partner and parent, too. All of these *Eight Elements* will also spill into your personal life. If you haven't already, you're going to start recognizing how your emotional feelings effect your performance at work and in everything you do in your life."

I hope Sanjay is listening to the call, Susan thought.

"Hopefully by the end of this session, you are going to realize you have a choice of how and when you express your emotions and your reactions. In every moment we have a choice to take control of how we feel about a situation. We can't always change a situation, but we can change how we react to it.

"You see, self-awareness and emotional intelligence is the

understanding of *you*...what you do and why you do it. According to Daniel Goleman, Emotional Intelligence Expert and Author, *The Five Domains of Emotional Intelligence* are:

1. Knowing your emotions
2. Managing your own emotions
3. Motivating yourself
4. Recognizing and understanding other people's emotions
5. Managing relationships and the emotions of others

"Goleman asserts that emotional competencies are the best differentiators between star performers and typical performers. Compelling leaders know how to "get real" with themselves, by identifying their own negative emotional patterns and being able to instantly take control over any reactivity they may be feeling in the moment. When you are self-aware, you do not react...but rather, you observe the situation objectively—leaving your own emotional reactivity out of the observation."

A memory from Susan's first job suddenly drifted to the surface. Susan had sobbed in her manager's office in frustration over some silly tiff with a co-worker. Thinking about it, Susan blushed. That manager had been a saint to not only put up with that, but to empathize and encourage her as well.

"Emotional self-control happens in the present moment; and "emotional self-management," as Goleman calls it, is the hallmark of a compelling leader.

"When you have self-awareness and emotional intelligence, you are more conscious of your impact on others and of their perceptions of you. Compelling leaders can sense and feel the emotions of others and whether people are feeling comfortable around them. If people are not comfortable, self-aware leaders know how to make the necessary adjustments to put people at ease.

"Emotional sensitivity is so key to having self-awareness. When you're emotionally sensitive to your own emotions and to those of others, you'll start noticing your impact on people.

"This also works in reverse. Other people bring their negativity, their bad moods and their low state of mind to interactions. As you increase your emotional sensitivity, you'll start to notice and think, 'That person feels really negative to me today. I wonder what's going on with them.'"

It suddenly occurred to Susan that maybe something was going on with Sanjay, completely separate from their marriage. *Maybe Sanjay is having a bad week.* Susan felt curious about what event might have occurred in her husband's life, and a little ashamed that she hadn't even considered this before.

"Keep in mind that sometimes someone else's low emotional state triggers a low emotional state within us. For example, I called a friend of mine over the weekend, and unbeknownst to me I caught her at a really bad time as she was dealing with an elderly father and a lot of issues concerning his health and well-being.

"I took her low state of mind, personally. I kept thinking, 'What's wrong with her? What did I do to upset her? Why isn't she relating to me the same way that she usually does?' It wasn't until late in the call she told me about her dad. Before she told me what was going on, I made it all about me, as we so often do. Emotional sensitivity can open you up to how others feel; and in our next session, Element Three will demonstrate the importance of empathy to your personal brand.

Everything Ellen was saying was clicking with Susan. Something was up with Sanjay and it was dragging down their relationship. Even the kids had seemed subdued. She wondered how she would be able to talk to him about it without sounding like she was attacking or blaming him.

"Sometimes, just one insight about your life and how you operate in the world, or how you impact others, can reorganize the way you're showing up in a very profound way. I believe that when we understand ourselves fully we can show up almost any way we choose to. And we can have a lot more self-control in the moment if things become too intense.

"Self-aware leaders know that the way they do *everything* matters... and controlling their emotional behavior, maintaining a positive state of mind and having a sense of self-accountability are the things that put other people at ease. Tony Robbins says that, "The way you make people feel, influences their purchase decisions. And people will never buy into doubt or uncertainty...their own or yours.""

"When you have self-awareness, you can: Sense when people are not comfortable with you (they might be feeling nervous, bored or distracted). And you can get others to drop their guard by getting curious about how they are feeling, and why.

"Instead of trying to get people to feel comfortable around you, work on becoming a person who's comfortable to be with."

Wow! Susan thought as she jotted down 'comfortable to be with.' She looked at her surveys again and it all clicked! This was the missing key ingredient! These people weren't comfortable with her, because she was trying too hard to make them like her and feel comfortable about entrusting their financial planning to her! And who wants to be around someone like that?

Susan put down her pen and laughed to herself. It was that simple. On the phone, the session was wrapping up. She picked up her phone and texted Sanjay.

"That was really good. How do you feel?"

After a few moments pause, the reply buzzed through of, "I think it was the right message at the right time."

"What does that mean?" she asked.

There was no reply.

Chapter Four

Element #3: Artfully Communicate

"Hey, Susan?" the voice of the office assistant called her back from her thoughts.

"Yes?"

"I think you need to call the Browns."

"Did I miss a call?" Susan had been staring at her cell waiting for Sanjay to text back. Had she missed a call on the office line?

"Um, no," the assistant squirmed. "We just got paperwork that they are pulling their funds and going to a different wire house."

"What?" Susan's heartbeat pounded in her chest. The Browns were good clients and she had held their account for years. There had been no hint of a problem!

"If you can call right away, you might be able to change their mind..." the assistant's voice trailed off. Almost no one changed their minds at this stage. They had already signed and filed the paperwork with one of Susan's competitors.

"Thanks," Susan grabbed her phone and looked pointedly at the door. The assistant beat a hasty retreat, closing the door behind her.

But as soon as the door clicked shut, Susan let go of the phone. She was breathing fast and shallow and wondered if this was what a panic attack felt like. The Brown's funds accounted for almost 10% of her assets under management. It wasn't her largest account, but it was still a severe blow.

Susan grabbed the employee handbook with the annual production goals. With the subtraction of the Brown account, she was at a deficit for assets under management for this year. Susan fought for control as the reality crashed in on her. She was suddenly behind, in danger of losing her position and about to break down and cry in the office.

What had happened? She pulled up her files and started looking at the performance and communication records for the Brown account. It was performing well. Maybe she could have called more often?

Was it over friendliness? One of Susan's survey's had hinted at that.

1. How did you come to work with Susan?

Susan was referred to us by a good friend, who got great results from Susan's financial consulting.

2. What was your overall impression of Susan and her work?

Overall, Susan was open, honest and easy to work with. Her customized and very detailed financial plan helped lessen the overwhelm we were feeling financially. But my husband initially had some issues with her over-the-top friendliness and didn't want to hire her...but now, he's very glad we did.

3. What were the major benefits you received from working with Susan?

Greatest benefits from working with Susan: she helped us eliminate our debt over time, as well as increase our savings (thus helping us take more control over what had been super-stressful).

4. How could Susan have improved her work product and your experience of working with her?

Areas for improvement: My husband had a much harder time trusting Susan's ability to really grow our assets and create a college fund for the kids (although she has done a great job at that!)...But initially, he thought she was too chatty and focused on getting him to like her and becoming a family friend, than on sharing the strengths and benefits of her program, re: how she would tangibly help us get out of our financial mess.

5. How would you describe your experience with Susan to someone else in need of these services?

Susan is a fabulous Financial Planner and I highly recommend her! She helped us save money, rather effortlessly (without even thinking about it), by providing a detailed plan of action for getting us out of debt and for overcoming our self-defeating financial behaviors.

6. What three adjectives would you use to describe Susan?

Smart, Personable, Genuine

Could over-friendliness ruin a good relationship? There was only one way to find out. She grit her teeth and picked up the phone.

After two rings the call went straight to voicemail. Susan hung up, swept over by a wave of dread that she had lost the account and relief that they hadn't answered the phone, thus avoiding a confrontation.

What is wrong with me? Susan scolded herself. Her eyes wandered her desk until they latched onto the notes from the personal branding conference call. Phrases that popped out were 'emotional intelligence,' 'get real' and 'observe your emotions.' Suddenly Susan became acutely aware of her emotions, and the reactions resulting from her turmoil.

Feeling bolder, she picked up the phone and dialed again. This time the phone went straight to voicemail.

"Hello Mr. and Mrs. Brown. I am terribly sorry to see that you are leaving my practice. Your account is and has been very important to me. I'd like a chance to understand how I could have better served you. I'm going to be sending you a survey in the mail. If you could please take a moment to fill it out and return it, I would really appreciate it. I wish you all the best. Thank you."

Before she could think twice about it, Susan wrote a personalized note to Mr. and Mrs. Brown, attached the survey and sent it out in the afternoon mail.

* * *

Sanjay showed up to the conference room first and snagged the best chair at the table. If he was going to be uncomfortable, sitting next to people who may or may not hate him, he was at least going to have a place to put his notepad and the good chair that didn't tilt at an odd angle.

The surveys had not all been horrible. In fact, everyone seemed to think that his contributions to the team were significant, even hinting that he should take more credit for his innovative work. Yet, there had been a running theme of abruptness, cold behavior, and not feeling heard. A female co-worker said that last one, it was like Susan's voice reading that survey response.

Things were still tense at home. The kids were good, but Susan had been unusually quiet. He missed her talking and sharing about her day. He wished he knew how to get her to open up to him.

The room filled up quickly as the time for the personal branding webinar grew near. Some co-workers made a stab at conversation. Sanjay mostly just doodled and waited for the conference call to start.

"Welcome everyone to the third of eight sessions on personal branding and influence-building!" Ellen began. "It's been a couple weeks since your Personal Impact Surveys went out. If you put a two-week deadline on the survey, you should have your responses back by now. The next step is to assess the responses to each question.

"You're only the best at what you do if the people you serve think you're the best at what you do. And that's because value is only a perception. But the good news is that all perceptions can be managed. If you don't like the feedback you're getting from your Personal Impact Surveys, pat yourself on the back for having the courage to take this program and invest in yourself and in your own career destiny."

I wish this felt like bravery, Sanjay thought. It felt more like a sucker punch.

"Realize that this is the right time to change and manage the perceptions that you want people to have of you. Brand-building is all about creating and managing the way you want people to think of you and your work."

"Quick question, Ellen," a male voice interrupted. "What if I didn't get all of my surveys back?"

"This happens. Life gets busy for all of us. If anyone did not promptly respond, contact them to encourage a response. Make sure you emphasize how much their feedback means to you.

"If you feel like you are pestering that person by contacting them, remember, responses to each question will give you information that will help you articulate your brand, in terms of your benefits, your work value and your personal value.

"I have a question too, Ellen," a female voice piped in. "My feedback was really generic and positive. I'm not saying I don't have room for improvement, I know I do. But no one is telling me what that area might be. What should I do?"

If only this was my problem, Sanjay thought. *It was like they were waiting for the opportunity to tell me what they really thought!*

"It's really good that you recognize this as a problem," Ellen praised. "It would be so easy to say 'I'm perfect!' and walk away. I think the way you build a really compelling personal brand is to make lemonade out of the lemons. If your feedback is only positive, it might be beneficial to get together with some of these people. Go have lunch or a cup of coffee, or call them on the phone if they're not in your vicinity. Tell them how much you appreciated the feedback they gave you. Then say, you were curious why they didn't answer the question, re: how could you improve their service.

"If they wrote, 'you're terrific the way you are. There's no room for improvement.' I would try to pull something out of them. Usually you can. Dig a little deeper, so you can debrief their candid feedback and rebuild your personal brand in a way that you suits you.

"Once you have debriefed all of the responses to your surveys, it's time to assess the difference between how you want to be perceived, versus how people currently perceive you. What gaps are there? What can you do to close the gaps? At this point in the process, it's important to be impeccably honest with yourself.

"For example, one of your brand attributes might be your ability to collaborate with all types of people; yet no one mentioned 'collaboration' in your survey feedback. Or maybe instead of no mention of collaboration, it is implied that you are actually difficult to work with.

"In this situation there would be a huge gap between the way you are and the way you want to be perceived. But it isn't the end of the world! In fact, this is not terrible at all. If the people that you most want to influence do not see you as a collaborator, that's fine. Because these 'value gaps' can actually be managed. You can turn that around and get the word out that you are, in fact, a great collaborator.

"Does anyone want to share a similar experience?"

"Yes, Ellen," a female voice volunteered. "This is Shante from HP calling in from Kenya; and this was exactly my experience. I found that what I wanted people to perceive in me was very different from the feedback that I received. There were real gaps in key things that I want my brand to be known for in the future.

"For example, my communication skills. I really thought that they were good. But nowhere in the survey responses was a mention of my communication skills. Am I a failure?"

I'm not the only one shocked by their results! Another thought quickly followed the first one, *Wow, she is brave to share that!*

"Of course not, Shante!" Ellen exclaimed. "You are absolutely not a failure! Obviously for some reason, your communication was not something your respondents highlighted about your personal brand; but this silence isn't necessarily a condemnation.

"In your case, it makes sense to follow up with your survey

respondents and ask specifically about your communication. It could be that you communicate so well that no one thought to add it. Or it could be a real gap. You won't know until you ask!

"The fact is, Shante, you need to ask and find out, because you can read anything into the silence. For the other listeners on the call, if this is your situation, have a casual conversation with your respondents individually. Point out to people how effective communication (or whatever the attribute in question is), is important to you. Nudge people a little bit and ask for more of their candid feedback. This can also open the door to other feedback they might have withheld in the first round."

Maybe I could ask David about his responses, Sanjay considered. *He seems like he won't be over-emotional.*

"The Personal Impact Surveys are not just an exercise to see how you are being perceived. We will later turn those survey responses into raving testimonials. These testimonials (with permission) can be used to promote and talk about your work. If one is particularly good, you might even want to ask that respondent to add their testimonial to your LinkedIn profile. That verifiable value means that you aren't just talk. Your value is tangible and has actually been verified.

"Take particular note of what others consider to be the greatest benefit you provide. Highlight raving compliments and accolades, as well as active adjectives that appear within the answers. Finally, identify ways you can improve your impact through professional growth and personal brand clarity."

Sanjay thought a bit about his surveys. *There are some compliments in there,* he decided. *I can do this.*

"I have a client from the UK, that works at Cisco. She was in her office on a normal day, and there was an unfamiliar man who was in the hallway, and he stopped her and asked her a question, and they got to talking. It turned out that he was from corporate headquarters in San Jose, California and he was visiting the UK for a meeting.

"This executive asked MJ, "What do you do here in the UK for Cisco?" Well, because of having integrated all of the *Eight Elements of Influence,* MJ knew how to tell a compelling story about her value. Using the positive sound bites that she deconstructed from the Personal Impact Surveys, MJ was able to effectively communicate her unique value and passionately tell her story, right there, on the spot.

"The executive was so blown away by the way she told her brand story of value, that he invited her to come to California, all expenses paid, for one week, to take part in a special, high-level project, as an expert from her department. It actually changed her whole career and took MJ to a whole new level.

"Being able to articulate her brand story by sharing some 3rd-party testimonials of the value she brought to other people, and thus to Cisco's bottom line, got MJ noticed by a work team that she would have never had any influence over, otherwise. And, in doing so, it put her in a new league throughout the company."

Susan told me that she met that lady at Ellen's Commonwealth Club talk! Somehow knowing that the story was 100% true, made Sanjay feel better about this whole process. *If it helped her visibility and success, it can help me.*

"People want to experience a feeling before they listen to the facts... they need to like and trust you (in their right brain), before they want to engage with the tangible facts (in their left brain). All choices and buying decisions are first made *emotionally*—we want to get a positive feeling first, in our emotional right brain, before listening and taking in all of the facts. Later, those positive feelings get *justified* logically in the left brain—because we also want the facts.

"Let's say you're on a job interview, or you're in a performance review. You want to first connect emotionally. And once that all-important emotional connection is made, then you need to logically justify, with facts, why they should hire you or promote you.

"By engaging others with thought-provoking questions, telling compelling stories that illustrate your value, and intentionally listening to others without pre-set expectations, you can quickly connect emotionally and build meaningful rapport with others.

"The third of the *Eight Elements* is Artfully Communicate. By the end of this session you should be able to build rapport quickly, illustrate your value with story telling and engage people with your active listening skills."

Storytelling. Sanjay thought. *Sounds like bragging about how great I am. And that's something I am definitely not willing to do!*

"Mindful communication, in general, builds trust and rapport—it puts people at ease, so they want to open up to you. Part of building rapport is to find things in common and be authentically interested in the people around you.

"We can do that by talking to them and finding common ground. Usually it's better to build rapport around non-business topics if we can, just because people tend to like people who seem similar to them.

"So if you're a gardener and you're talking to another gardener, or you're an avid reader or an adventure traveler, or you're a dog lover, find common ground. Engage others with thought-provoking questions. People love to talk about themselves and answer your questions."

Sanjay looked around the table. *Probably the only thing I have in common with any of these people is the job.*

"Ellen?" a man's voice jumped in. "I'm giving a presentation to a group of executives. How do I build rapport with a larger audience?"

"Good question!" Ellen replied. "When you start a presentation, most people launch right into their first slide. Instead, take a moment. Spend some unofficial time building an emotional connection with your audience. Thank them for being there, for investing their time, ask them an opening question to instantly engage them, or share any other sincere feelings that seem appropriate.

"If you have the time, always tell a story. Stories create an instant emotional connection. By telling a story, you can genuinely break down the barriers between yourself and your audience, thus creating an emotional connection, before launching into a logical, factual presentation.

"According to the best-selling "Compelling People" book's research, 'the two rhetorical forms that naturally project strength and warmth together are stories and humor (two critical ingredients for a successful talk, and a compelling personal brand). Our brains are wired for stories, and everyone likes them. It turns out that story-telling relaxes our critical faculties and lowers our guard. And in that respect, sharing a story is an inherently warm experience. The ability to tell a good story is a display of competence and stories can persuade us to follow leaders, invest our savings, vote for a candidate, or support a good cause.' That is strength. Does that help?"

"Yes, that's perfect! Thanks!"

"In addition to sharing a great story, you must *actively* listen in the present moment to the people around you. At any given time in our very distracted world, most people are only half-listening to a conversation. Many think they already know what you are going to say. But when you are truly present, you do not compare what someone is telling you with what you think you already know!

"Conventional listening is when you are involved in a conversation, but you are paying more attention to the internal voice in your head. This voice listens with its own agenda, is often running background commentary and is constantly comparing notes."

Sanjay's ears perked up. Something just clicked and made him think of Susan. He paid closer attention as Ellen continued.

"By contrast, actively listening in the present moment and hearing something new, without any judgment or analysis and empathetically echoing back to the other person that you 'get' them, will appeal to both their logic and their emotion.

"In addition to withholding judgment or analysis, there are two more components to actively listening in the present moment. The first is listening with curiosity. Being genuinely engaged in what is going on around you. The second component is to echo empathy. That's when you say, "I'm so sorry that happened to you," Or "I can't even imagine what that is like." It is listening and validating the person speaking, on an emotional level."

Wow! Sanjay felt a huge puzzle piece in his life suddenly drop into place. His heart started beating overtime as the listening implications struck home. *Susan doesn't feel like I'm engaged. Maybe nobody does.*

"When you're not present, people feel disconnected. When you are listening in the present moment, people feel heard and seen. If people feel seen and heard, it creates a genuine connection and paves the way to deeper rapport. If you are present, you can learn a lot about someone and gain a much better understanding of his/her unique, personal reality.

"Bypassing our own busy thinking and listening to others with a sense of insatiable curiosity makes time stand still. When we become present, we gain access into our own intuitive wisdom and we gain important insight into the other person's version of reality.

"When you can reflect back what's in someone's head, they feel as if they were really heard and valued by you. People can *feel* your presence and know when you're really with them. Likewise, they can also tell when you are not present or when you have "checked out" of the conversation. Instead of trying to really listen to someone, learn to recognize when you're *not* listening fully.

"Great storytelling illustrates the value of your personal brand with emotion and logic. When someone asks about what you do, share the experience of your value and the value of your experience in the form of a story. Instead of listing your accomplishments, tell stories of real-life situations that illustrate the value you have brought to others and the passion that guides your work.

"Typical selling involves demonstrating how your product or service would solve a problem. Storytelling puts the other person in the emotional position of feeling and sensing your value, because stories go directly into the right brain—their emotional center. They feel what it would be like if you were able to deliver the same result to them that you got for the person in your story. When you tell a story about your value, it has less to do with you, and more to do with how you delivered value to someone else.

"You can't tell a story without some emotional and sensory details. Stories capture people's imagination so much more quickly than a PowerPoint or any other objective information you can give someone."

Sanjay just let the words wash over him. He felt like he was going to have to go back and listen to the presentation another three times to get it all. Ellen was wrapping up the call, but Sanjay was still contemplating all that she said about actively listening. Susan was always saying that he was difficult to talk to. *Maybe, just maybe, I can make her feel like I'm listening. Like I care.*

Sanjay's phone buzzed with an incoming text. "Story Telling! I feel like this is going to transform my sales presentations!"

It was amazing to Sanjay that he and Susan could sit in the exact same meeting and get two completely different messages. Susan apparently had learned about sales techniques. Sanjay realized that this was his moment to get Susan talking to him again.

"Tell me more!" he replied.

Chapter Five

———

Element #4: Radiate Likeability and Empathy

Sanjay found himself back in the conference room less than an hour later, this time too late for his comfy chair, but early enough to have a place at the table. Susan had been blowing up his phone with thoughts about the personal branding webinar. So much so, that Sanjay only had time to digest the one little morsel that was helping him with his wife. Actively listen. That meant getting fully present, asking questions and listening to the answers. He wondered what would happen if he did more of that in this team meeting that Marty, his boss, had just scheduled.

Marty came in last and took the seat that had been held for him at the head of the table. The agenda was passed around, but a quick glance proved that most of the list was filled with stale, carry-over items from prior weeks.

Marty seemed to come to the same conclusion. "What is the agenda of this team?"

The room grew silent and uncomfortable.

"Nobody?" Marty took out a red pen and drew a giant 'X' over the content of the agenda.

David, who was sitting across from Sanjay, shifted slightly in his seat. Marty honed in on him.

"David, what is the purpose of this team?"

David cleared his throat, stalling for time. "The Innovation Lab is supposed to roll out new procedures and tools for the IT department?" David offered hesitantly.

"So why do we not have any new tools or procedures to implement? Why are we not innovating?"

David didn't respond this time. No one volunteered.

"Innovation requires great teamwork," Marty began to lecture; and teamwork is woefully lacking in this department."

Is this aimed at me? Sanjay wondered.

"Corporate America is not the place for the lone creative genius anymore. There are too many lone wolves on this team. A good team is about each one of you, individually, and your ability to communicate and collaborate with each other. Each of your individual contributions and ideas become even greater when they are shared and expanded on by the team.

"It is all about synergy. The concept that if I bring an idea to David, he can bring his expertise to bear on the issue. Then he could turn to Sanjay, or one of the many other experts on this team, and flesh it out further."

He would take his idea to someone else first, Sanjay agreed mentally. *And then he would bring it to me to get it done.*

"Each of you is here because you bring something unique to this team." Marty waved the defunct agenda, "This is not the Innovation Lab at it's best. This is not evidence of a team working together to get things done.

"All of these agenda items are dead," Marty declared. "From this moment on, we are only interested in new ideas, new concepts, new projects that we, as a team, can move forward on...*together*. All of our jobs are dependent on our ability to constantly innovate. Those who cannot innovate as part of a collaborative team have no place here."

The silence in the room was deafening. No one moved. Sanjay tried not to breathe.

"My first assignment for you, as a team, is to brainstorm ways to identify approaches to problems and solutions faster. This is going to be a group activity, so everyone is going to need to contribute an idea. No idea is open for debate until everyone has had a chance to offer one.

"Who is going to go first?"

The meeting went on. Every time Sanjay volunteered his thoughts, Marty met him with a sigh and a dismissal. *He hates me,* Sanjay thought. *Why does he have to make it so obvious?*

When the meeting finally came to an end, Marty pulled Sanjay aside. As they entered Marty's office, Sanjay felt very much like he had been called to the headmaster's office back in grade school. Marty and Sanjay sat on either side of the desk, staring at each other.

Finally, Marty cleared his throat. "If you were to choose a team, would you choose yourself to be a team member?"

Sanjay was perplexed, "Yes. Of course I would."

"I'm not sure that would be the case with your teammates. I'm not sure that they would pick you."

Sanjay felt a stab of panic in his gut. He was horrified. Was he about to be fired?

"You are not the only lone wolf on this team," Marty told him. "I could tell during the meeting that you thought it was 100% about you, and it's not. However, like most lone wolves, you think everything is about you. The problem is, you work on a team."

"What do you want me to do?"

"Get out of your cubicle, for one. I want to see you succeed on this team, Sanjay. You have great ideas, great drive. You see projects through to completion. I could see you being an Innovation Lab team leader one day. However, you don't always appreciate and value the contributions of others. You can be dismissive of their ideas, quick to judge, and often very abrupt. You won't be able to lead until you can see the other members of your team as human *beings,* not human *doings,* to borrow Ellen's phrase.

"How do you feel you are doing with the personal branding program?"

Sanjay thought for a moment. "I am trying to work on my active listening skills."

"Good," Marty said. "Keep going. Keep learning. I think that you have great potential and there's a huge opportunity to learn here."

"Thank you," Sanjay told the desk, looking down sheepishly.

"I'm serious though," Marty warned as he stood up to dismiss him. "Get out of your cubicle. Get to know your teammates, communicate and collaborate more."

* * *

Susan had her survey results laid out on her desk. Keywords and phrases were highlighted and circled for emphasis. The eLearning course had been hard, but she had finally embraced the process, both the good comments and the well-meaning criticism. She was actually surprised by how hopeful and light-hearted she felt. Now that the initial sting of the feedback had faded, she could see the wisdom in knowing where she was, in order to plan where she was going.

Just then, the hold music for the webinar conference call faded into Ellen's voice. Susan clicked up the volume, looking forward to this week's lesson.

"Good Morning! Welcome to the fourth session of the series! I'm so happy to be here with you today, as the upcoming Element is very important. The fourth Element is to Radiate Likeability and Empathy. But before we launch into that, we need to have a quick check in.

"Would anyone like to share any thoughts or experiences they've had so far on the *Eight Elements?*"

"Yes, this is Katya, and I'm a Systems Engineer from the Czech Republic. The industry I work in is typically male-dominated. As a woman,

I naturally recognize and share feelings and experiences. I relate with other women at work more than with the men. When I really began to see changes from this program was when I focused on the active listening Element, (when you told us to find something in common with our team members, outside of work). I've been establishing new connections with my co-workers that don't necessarily have to do with what we do at work, on a day-to-day basis; and the connecting feels more at a human level. For example, I just learned that our team leader is also a foster parent like me; and now we have so much more to share about our foster kids and their progress."

"That's amazing!" Ellen said. "Finding things in common is not just about making someone like you. It's also about opening up and sharing the things that make you unique. By building these human connections, not only do you start perceiving your co-workers as real people, but they start seeing you in a new way, too. Thank you so much for sharing, Katya.

"What about storytelling? Does anyone have something to share there?" Ellen prompted.

Susan was surprised to see her finger hit the "unmute" button. "Yes, Ellen? This is Susan from the San Francisco Bay Area," Susan shook her head ruefully. Why was she so nervous? "I'm really struggling with the storytelling. I believe that it works; and I can see it in your presentations. It just doesn't sound natural coming out of my mouth. It sounds rehearsed and cheesy."

"I get that, especially if you aren't used to telling stories," Ellen acknowledged. "If you are just putting your story together, it might sound overly prepared, or canned. But with time, you will get much better at it and your stories will sound less rehearsed and much more natural and authentic."

Susan jotted down "authenticity" and re-muted her phone. She felt almost winded from just talking on the phone. Sharing with strangers was hard!

"On that note, we are going to launch into how to be perceived as an expert by those people you most want to influence. Positioning yourself as an expert in your field involves translating your experience and skillset into tangible benefits that people want and appreciate. To re-brand yourself as an influential professional with whom others want to work, you sometimes need to re-translate, re-position and re-package your talents and experience. Positioning and packaging your expertise is the cornerstone for having an effective personal brand.

"In this session, you will assess your relevant experience and value. This information will give you what you need to articulate your benefits in a compelling way.

"So, how do you differentiate yourself? This is often a black hole for a lot of professional people. They say, 'I'm really not any different. There's tons of people at my company (or out in the business world) that do what I do.' Well, I would beg to differ; and you will see that I'm right, as you dig into the process.

"Your Personal Impact Survey results revealed how people perceive you; and if you look closely, you will see that there are probably differences in the five people's perceptions. So you're already differentiating yourself whether you know it or not; and this process will help you to define that even more clearly. But like it or not, you're also seeing lots of commonality in the feedback; so pay careful attention there as well.

"So what are you known for knowing? This is a million-dollar question for most. What makes you special? What's your 'secret sauce?' What is your contribution to your company's brand? What's your Return on Investment (ROI)? What's the company receiving in exchange for your paycheck? Or, if you work on your own, what are you known for knowing becomes more critical a question to clearly and succinctly answer, as you and your business/service are really one and the same brand. So, take a moment to think about these two questions. Write down your thoughts.

"Perhaps you've been called something that distinguishes you, something you can quote that you're known for. Maybe a manager once gave you a moniker that you're the "leader in [blank]" or the "expert at [blank]." If someone else said it, you can quote them. But you can't just make one up and call yourself that. That's not genuine.

"So what are you an expert in, or on the way to becoming an expert at? Or what do you want to be known as an expert at? This is a time to think through all of those things, so you'll have much more to contribute right away. And think ahead. Think aspirationally, too, about how you want to be known a few years from now, or at the end of your career; and start building that personal brand equity right now.

I'm an expert at working with professional women and young families. I help them grow their assets, reduce debt, save for the future; and I give them peace of mind knowing that their finances are in expert hands. Susan smiled to herself. That had been so hard less than a month ago!

"In the business framework, core competencies are a combination of skills, knowledge and personal attributes. From your client's perspective, core competencies are the benefits they receive from your services and your deliverables. Everyone wants to know *what's in it for me* before they commit to working with you. We only care about something when it becomes personal and fills a gap or need we have.

"For those of you who are struggling with the storytelling assignment from last week, this might be another way to approach it. Think about what you do and an outcome or result of your work. How did you achieve the desired outcome for a client? How did that client benefit from your work? If you can articulate it in a personal and succinct way, you'll be able to build a compelling story around that experience.

Eureka! Susan thought. She could create *sound bites* from the survey results, but the real story was her clients. She could keep them anonymous, but she had absolutely brought many a benefit to most of her clients. Susan felt a huge weight lift off of her shoulders.

"It's no coincidence," Ellen continued, "that we call people we like and feel good about 'attractive.' Most attractive people are confident, positive, comfortable in their own skin, open, authentic and likeable. The most important component to likeability is empathy. Empathy means being able to sense others' feelings and take an active interest in their concerns. When people sense your empathy, they are more likely to feel comfortable, open up to you, like you and want to do business with you.

"Never underestimate the power of likeability. According to Tim Sanders, author of "The Likeability Factor," there are *Four Keys to Likeability*. If you possess all Four Keys, you're much more likely to build instant trust and rapport and thus, influence others.

"The first of the *Four Keys to Likeability* is Friendliness, which is the feeling of liking for another person and enjoying their company. The second key is Relevance, the pertinence or a connection to the matter at hand. The third key to likeability is Empathy or the capacity to recognize and share feelings experienced by another person. The final key is Realness—being yourself instead of trying to be someone you're not."

Susan had hastily written down each of the Four Keys. The last one struck a nerve. Realness. She underlined it for emphasis. Then in bold letters wrote "BE REAL." *It's all clicking today.* Susan smiled.

"Leaders need people skills. I work a lot with technical people and so-called introverts. I work a lot with engineers, R&D people, financial analysts, and with people who usually put much more emphasis on their technical competencies than on their people skills. But research has shown that to move ahead in your career, it is more about your people skills and your ability to communicate and collaborate, and less about your technical competency. Your technical competency got you the job, but it's your people skills that will keep you there and help you thrive!

For the first time all session, Susan thought of Sanjay. She wondered how he was doing in this program. He had been aloof the last few days.

"Radiating Likeability and Empathy is about becoming more of who you really are," Ellen continued. "It's *not* about trying to emulate the qualities you admire in someone else. Some people think, 'Wow! I think I'll try to be more like (fill in the blank). She does this, that, and the other thing, and I'll just copy her.' It doesn't work that way. The type of combined strength and warmth that I am recommending that you inject into everything you do, is less about what you're doing and more about who you're *being*.

"Warmth radiates from influential people who are at ease with themselves. It's an energetic by-product of empathy and compassion; and people can actually *feel* your warmth (or not). Warm people feel authentically present and extra-human. Like empathy, warmth involves understanding the emotional state of an individual and seeing the best in them. Warm people generate more emotional sensitivity towards others, manifesting as an energy of unconditional acceptance, that feels very real, open, accessible and safe to be around.

"When feelings of warmth are created, people naturally open up more, making it easier to build immediate trust and rapport. Body language has a lot to do with projecting warmth; and a genuine smile and a positive intention (communicated through your eyes) makes the warmth believable. And just like so many other components, warmth can never be faked.

Susan thought about her client list. The ones she felt most comfortable with were the ones she had let down her professional persona with. She felt genuinely herself when she was working with them. But, she had never been real with the Browns; and because she was so hyper-focused on being liked, they didn't take her expertise seriously. This realization made her feel sad. If only she had known earlier!

"Friendliness and relevance are closely related to another *Element of Influence*. Friendliness comes directly from your self-awareness. It's about understanding your impact on others and making the necessary adjustments.

"People listen more effectively when your message is relevant and of interest to them, so it's important to qualify people's needs and to only express and communicate what is relevant to their situation. If you or what you have to offer isn't relevant, there's less chance of people taking the time to like you. People tend to give their attention to those who "fit" into their world or who have a "solution" to offer them.

"The ability to feel empathy is directly related to your ability to acknowledge and identify your own feelings. If you haven't felt these feelings yourself, it will be very difficult to understand how someone else is feeling.

Not a problem, Susan chuckled to herself. She knew the chaos and frustration of young kids, balancing the needs of today with the wants for the future. She knew about comforting a child at 3am and still going to work at 6am. *I can do this.*

The cellphone on her desk buzzed, startling Susan, Sanjay usually never texted her first. "I think I'm struggling with empathy."

Holy cow. Susan bit her lip, trying to come up with an appropriate response. Finally she settled for the truth.

"We can talk about it tonight. Did I mention I love you?"

Chapter Six

Element #5: Inspire Confidence

The kids were in bed, if not yet quite asleep. The television was off, and Sanjay and Susan each cradled a glass of wine on the couch. After a prolonged silence, Susan finally broke the ice.

"What's going on?"

Sanjay studied his wine glass. "This whole personal branding thing has been a lot tougher than I thought."

Susan could certainly agree, and was tempted to regale him with stories of her own journey. But something told her that Sanjay needed to get something off his chest. She decided to pry. "How so?"

"I wasn't actively listening in the present moment," his eyes flickered to Susan and back to his glass. "Not to you, not to the people at work."

Susan's heart hurt for him. She wanted to tell him that he was wrong, reassure him that he had been a good husband. But he didn't listen, not consistently and sometimes his responses were just...wrong. Thankfully, Sanjay wasn't needing a response just yet.

"I tried listening. After that session on listening, it seems like that was all I did for a week. Just listen." His eyebrows narrowed, "It didn't make anything better though."

"What are you trying to make better?" Susan asked.

Sanjay got up and retrieved a folder from the table. He handed it to her without a word.

Susan didn't know what was inside of the folder, but she certainly didn't expect to find Sanjay's Personal Impact Surveys. She scanned through them quickly, trying to glean why Sanjay was so upset.

"They all hate me."

"No!" Susan objected. She pointed to a comment. "See? This person says that you are very intelligent and focused on getting the job done."

"It also says that I'm abrupt and quick to judge," Sanjay countered, not even looking at the page she held up.

A quick glance through the rest of the surveys revealed that Sanjay was right. Had he memorized all of his results? She rifled through the papers, hoping for something to say.

"You said I was hard to talk to." Sanjay's voice had gone weirdly flat.

"Sometimes you are. Sometimes it's like you're missing that part in the conversation where you acknowledge the other person's feelings. You're already onto the next step where you fix their problems. "But Sanjay," she reached out for his hand, I still love you."

"Why?"

"Why?" Susan couldn't believe he could even question this. "Because you are my other half. You keep me grounded. You support me when I'm down. You are the father of our children. You are the person that I want to see at the end of the day."

"But I don't listen or acknowledge your feelings."

Susan thought for a moment. "Do you remember that time when I was studying for my Financial Planner certification, and I had that total freak out moment, and everything was really dramatic and over the top? Do you remember what you said to me?"

"No, I don't."

For the first time in the conversation, Sanjay sounded interested, even curious. Susan took hope from that, grabbed his shoulders and firmly said, "Snap out of it!"

Sanjay's eyes met hers in shock.

"That's what you told me. Snap out of it," Susan whispered. "And now I'm telling you." Then she leaned forward and brushed her lips against his.

"Taking an honest inventory of your uniqueness and value isn't supposed to be easy. I've been thrown for a loop myself. My feedback said that clients weren't taking me seriously. That I was sabotaging my meetings by trying to be over-the-top friendly. As Ellen would say, I was being incongruent. I'm still working on that."

"Too friendly?" Sanjay asked dumbfounded, as he found it so hard to be friendly, at all!.

"Yep," Susan smiled reassuringly. "It hurt, but it wasn't the end of the world. Remember, this is the starting point. The finish is wherever we decide we want it to be. "We can *proactively* manage the perceptions that people have of us" Susan reminded him." You can overcome these obstacles."

"Really?" Sanjay asked Susan hopefully.

"Really," she said firmly. "And just because you care this much about it."

It wasn't until Susan was falling into bed, after they had talked for hours and finished the bottle of wine, that Susan was able to put her finger on what was so remarkable about the night. For once, she had been Sanjay's rock. She provided the needed strength and was able to support him, after all the times he had her back. Susan knew her husband was hurting, but she also knew how determined he was to change things. She fell asleep with a smile, confident that they could handle the future together.

Sanjay sat at home on the couch in the middle of the afternoon. His youngest, Lily had to be picked up from daycare early with a fever. She was down for a nap now, and Sanjay was pleased that he would be able to call in live to the personal branding conference call.

He actually wished he *was* at work. Sanjay had been completely surprised how much talking to Susan had helped him. He hadn't realized what a funk he had worked himself into over this whole personal branding process. Things were really improving at the office. Susan had taught him a technique for making people feel heard, and so far the response had been fantastic. People were starting to warm up to him and open up more.

According to Susan, the trick to making people feel heard was to slow down and get fully present. Don't respond right away. A conversation is not a ping-pong ball shooting back and forth across the table. Susan had coached him to take a full breath and make eye contact before saying anything.

She had taught him that the second step was to acknowledge what he heard or how the other person might be feeling. He was still working on that part. So far he tended to repeat what he had heard in his own words, but he thought he might be able to spot the feelings a little better in the future.

For now, it was getting the results that he needed. He felt hopeful again.

"Hello and welcome to week five of the personal branding and influence-building program," Ellen greeted her audience. "Today I will be talking about my Fifth Element: Inspire Confidence.

"But I do want to take a moment to congratulate you on making it halfway through the program. You are sticking with it, and for that, I thank you and I suspect your career will thank you, too.

"Let me remind you, that your personal brand should answer the following:

What you're known for, what you're known as and what you're known for knowing. And as your career progresses, these things will also change and evolve.

"Let's jump into today's lesson, Element Five: Inspire Confidence. Confident people inspire the confidence of others; and it's impossible to be an effective leader without it. People *feel* your confidence (or your lack of it)! You cannot fake confidence...real confidence comes from deep inside of you; it's a way of *being* versus something that you *do*. All four of the previous Elements build confidence; as confidence is born out of self-awareness, realness, personal appreciation and self-understanding. And most importantly, remember that:

Confidence is the #1 reason people choose or buy anything!

"When you are in a positive state of mind, you project greater confidence. As a result, your self-confidence will inspire others around you. Self-confidence is an *attitude*, which helps create a positive and realistic perception of yourself and your abilities. Even though confidence is based on how you see your own uniqueness and intrinsic value as a person, confident people are not focused on themselves. They are fully present and in the moment; and when you're doing business with them, you feel like you're their most important client.

"The more faith you have in your own capabilities, the more you will be seen as confident. Being able to easily speak about your unique strengths, your special talents and the contribution your expertise brings to others, will make people have more confidence in you. If you lack confidence and do not believe in yourself, how can you convince anyone else of your value? You cannot affirm your uniqueness and value, the keys to successful personal branding and influence-building, if you don't value yourself."

To his own surprise, Sanjay's finger jumped over and unmuted his phone. *Am I really going to do this?*

"Ellen? This is Sanjay, an engineer, in the Silicon Valley. You might be able to tell from my voice that I am not from the US. In my country, we are not supposed to *toot our own horn*. It's just not considered appropriate in my culture. So, I'm really struggling with this aspect of the program."

"You know, I work with lots of different cultures from all around the world, so your situation is actually quite common, Ellen agreed. "However, to succeed, you are going to need to advocate for yourself and highlight your talents and the Return on Investment (ROI) your company gets from the contributions you are making to their bottom line. And that's where the art of storytelling is most useful. Your stories should focus on how you've helped someone else, and not on how fabulous you are.

"As you feel more confident, your verbal and non-verbal messages should reflect your own belief in what you do. When you really believe in what you do and the value you offer, your inner beliefs and self-assuredness will radiate through your non-verbal messages.

Sanjay considered his survey results for a moment. *Basically everyone said I needed to work on empathy and active listening.* He smiled wryly. *But at least I have consistency down!*

"When you experience insecurity...realize that it's only a state of mind; and you have bought into something about yourself that is not necessarily true. Confidence as we learned earlier, is nothing more than a state-of-mind; and so is self-doubt or insecurity.

"Feelings of self-doubt and low self-esteem are driven by fear. Whether it is not being good enough, not being valued or wanted, feeling worthless or insignificant. Your self-esteem is based on the opinion you have of yourself.

"Low self-esteem comes from the way we were treated in childhood or in important relationships. Through emotional exploration, compassion and self-education, we can heal the past and confidently move forward in life, leaving our emotional "baggage" from the past, in the past.

My self-esteem has really taken a beating lately, Sanjay thought.

"Confident people can accurately assess their capabilities and they have a deep faith in the future. Insecurity and self-doubt are the enemies of confidence. When you are feeling insecure, there are a few action steps you can take. These are the *Ten Tips for Building Confidence* (and for combating insecurity). Take particular note if one resonates with you.

"First, focus on your strengths and core competencies. Focusing on your core competencies builds confidence. Second, become more self-aware and try to understand where your self-doubt originally came from. Usually it stems from childhood or from an important relationship.

Grade school. Grade school was hell.

"Third, improve your posture and your physical appearance. The way you carry yourself tells a story that has a lot to do with how confident others perceive you to be. Fourth, admit your mistakes and weaknesses and learn from them. I think that this one is fairly self-evident.

Sanjay grinned, *Who me? I'm never wrong! Just don't ask my wife!*

"Fifth, consciously focus on the things that you are grateful for. Confident people focus on *gratitude.* Sixth, speak up and take risks. It's scary, but the more you do it, the more capable and confident you'll become.

Hmmm. Risks. He always delegated the risk taking to Susan. *Maybe,* he considered.

"Seventh, focus on what's in it *from* you...what you selflessly have to contribute to others. Eighth, practice being more enthusiastic about your accomplishments, your uniqueness and the value you bring to others. Some of us are so humble, that even when we choose to tell our story, it comes across as flat and unmemorable. So be sure to infuse your story with lots of enthusiasm.

Ellen said that for my benefit.

"Ninth, readily admit when you don't know something. Confident people know that they don't know everything, nor do they feel like they have to. The tenth and final item on our list is to take yourself and life less seriously. Develop a sense of humor and relax. Have fun with people."

Susan does tell me to lighten up. I guess I can give that a try.

"We are coming to the end of our Element on confidence...Both your self-confidence and also how confident others are about the value you have to offer them. However, there is an activity, in the Appendix, in the back of this book, called the "Influence Inquiry" that will help you take a closer look (from the inside-out), at how you convey confidence; and it will also help you to identify areas where you can build even more confidence. Through your honest answers, it will help you actually determine your confidence level in the workplace.

"The questions range from how confidently do you articulate your accomplishments? To what do you do very naturally in the workplace that appears deceptively easy from another's perspective? These questions are designed not only to tease out your weaknesses, but also to identify your strengths as well. I highly recommend that you take the time to answer these additional questions.

"I want to reiterate one more time, that a good personal brand exudes confidence and authenticity. To create that, you need to feel that, and part of that comes from really appreciating yourself; but you can't appreciate yourself if you are lying to yourself. So be real, dig in and do the exercises. Thanks so much for being on the call with me live today.

Appreciate myself? Sanjay knew the unconditional appreciation and love that he felt for his wife and his children. For his parents and siblings, too. But to appreciate himself that same way...Could he? *Did he?*

Chapter Seven

Element #6: Serve as a Leader

Susan tucked her *Ten Tips for Connecting Emotionally* notes under the sun visor and exited her car. These reminders were just part of the routine, but they gave her a boost before meetings. Today was a morning networking meeting of all the movers and shakers in her community. She was leaving nothing to chance.

With a bounce in her step and a smile on her face, Susan walked confidently into the meeting.

* * *

"Hey David, can I talk to you about something?"

David frowned at Sanjay. "I was going to have lunch before the branding webinar."

"Do you mind if I pick your brain while you eat?"

"Sure. Tag along."

Sanjay trusted David more than any of his other co-workers. He hoped David would be able to help him with his problem.

After they had grabbed chairs and food, David looked expectantly at Sanjay. "What's up?"

"I wanted to talk to you about the personal branding program," Sanjay began uncomfortably. When David didn't say anything, Sanjay struggled to continue. "It has been a bit more difficult than I first imagined it would be."

"Yes, I think we all are experiencing some growing pains," David offered sympathetically.

"Your feedback was helpful. I'm really working on my personal skills." Sanjay looked nervously at David, and he nodded in encouragement. "I'm having trouble with the storytelling thing and I was hoping you could help me with it."

David smiled kindly. "Which part is giving you trouble?"

Sanjay let out a breath he didn't realize he had been holding. David was going to help him.

* * *

Susan walked out of the networking meeting with a broad smile on her face. Her pocket was full of business cards and her calendar had three new appointments scheduled for next week—and they were all within her target market.

What's more, Susan felt really good about each and every one of her interactions. She really felt like she projected warmth, intelligence, strength and confidence in every conversation.

She texted Sanjay, "Walking on sunshine today! I rocked that meeting!"

To her surprise, he responded almost immediately.

"Good for you! I'm getting help from David on my storytelling. Talk to you after the branding call?"

Susan stopped in middle of the parking lot and re-read the text message. *Who are you and what have you done with my husband?* Grinning, she jumped into the car to get to the office before the next personal branding webinar started.

* * *

"Sorry about that," Sanjay said as he tucked his cellphone back in his pocket.

"No problem," David said between bites of sandwich. "Like I was saying, I think the story of the processor company would be perfect for you to share. You came up with a solution that no one else could, and you managed to get it implemented on time and on budget. That's a huge victory these days, you know that."

Sanjay hadn't ever considered the processor company. That project had seemed so effortless. It had never occurred to him that his story might not be filled with blood, sweat, and tears. It could just be the drama-free ease of getting a project done quickly and efficiently, and without any delays.

"I think you're onto something, David. It seems too easy, though. Was your story this simple?"

"Yes and no. Do you remember the networking project? The one you hated so much?"

Sanjay shuddered in memory of the sheer amount of data involved in that project.

"That's my story. I know you were miserable, but I excelled on that one. I hit my stride organizing all that data. The client was really pleased too." David shrugged. "Just because what we're good at seems effortless to others...that doesn't minimize our contribution to the team and to the bottom line."

"It's that easy," Sanjay said in awe. "Thank you, David. You have no idea how much you've helped me."

"No problem. Ready to tackle the next session?"

"Bring it on."

* * *

Susan plopped into her chair, slightly out of breath. She dialed into the call and heard the hold music. Whew! She had made it on time! Her initial appointment with a young woman had run a little long. It had been a fantastic meeting, but it left her in a rush to get back to the office.

A quick look at her calendar made Susan feel grateful. Class was over in two weeks. It had been an extremely helpful, even life-changing, program. However, life was changing rapidly as a result, as her schedule was filling up fast. Susan reflected on what a blessing this problem was.

Just then, Ellen's voice popped on the line. "Good morning and welcome to session six of the personal branding webinar series. Today we are going to be covering Element Six: Serve as a Leader. Serving as a leader is all about emotional self-control, so we are going to be diving into our personal experiences to identify how our subconscious reactions may be undermining or derailing our ability to lead.

"But I'm getting ahead of myself. Does anyone have thoughts, questions or realizations in regards to last week's session?" There was quiet on the line. "No one has anything to share?" Ellen prompted.

"I realized the whole confidence issue is prevalent in my workplace," a young woman's voice offered. "I work in the supply chain area, with a lot of men; but I originally came from a marketing background. Meetings normally have people talking over other people, being able to assert their opinions and direction.

"Sometimes I might have other ideas, but I'm more of an introvert; and I really have to force myself to more confidently put my ideas out there. I know I've struggled with that. I've asked questions, thinking that would help. But, I'm beginning to see that if I ask too many questions, it can undermine my authority and influence."

"You are certainly not the first to have this realization," Ellen acknowledged. "Confident people inspire the confidence of others. It's impossible to be an effective leader without confidence. People actually *feel* your confidence. It's a visceral thing. They feel your confidence, or your lack of it. It's also important to remember that you can't fake confidence. Real confidence isn't something you do. It's something that comes from deep inside of you. It's a way of *being*, versus something you can learn how to *do*.

"You can practice though. Practice does make perfect when it comes to confidence. Also, competence builds confidence, so this branding process should also be bolstering how competent you feel about your work.

"It doesn't seem like there were too many questions from last week," Ellen said after another pause, "so we are going to jump into our Sixth Element of Influence: Serve as a Leader. Leaders have congruence when what they say verbally and non-verbally match. So if you're feeling insecure, you can't fake acting like a confident leader. People can sense your insecurity, because you're lacking congruence between what you're saying and how we're feeling about you, from noticing your non-verbal cues.

"Leaders need to be in charge of their emotions. They cannot afford to have unconscious knee-jerk emotional reactions. When it comes to losing emotional self-control, men tend to have anger outbursts while women tend to get overly emotional and sometimes even cry. Neither one has a place in the workplace."

Yep, I'm a crier, Susan admitted to herself.

"Compelling leaders know how to effectively manage their impact on other people because they are extremely sensitive. They are in touch with their own emotions and sensitive to the emotions and reactions of others. Leaders possess a unique kind of people skills, which is more about having a "social sensitivity," giving them the ability to emotionally read most people and situations. According to Daniel Goleman, author and emotional intelligence expert, CEOs and Presidents are *seven times* more likely to be emotionally in control at all times.

"According to the *Portland Business Journal,* people skills are often described as: Understanding ourselves and moderating our responses. Talking effectively and *empathizing* accurately. Building relationships of trust, respect and productive interactions are all valuable outcomes of having people skills."

Crying had always embarrassed Susan as a show of weakness. For the first time, she also considered it as a barrier to her career success.

"Compelling leaders are present and in the moment. Therefore, they are extremely sensitive to their surroundings. They know that if they're not in the present moment with people, then they're not really in relationship with them. Their so-called "people skills" come from their sensitivity to the emotions and needs of others. Leaders are empathetic and they instantly *feel* important emotional info about someone and their situation.

"The ability to feel empathy is directly related to your ability to feel your own feelings and be able to identify them. If you haven't experienced these emotions yourself, it will be very difficult to understand how someone else is feeling. Therefore, the leaders who experience the widest and most varied range of emotions in themselves (both positive and negative), are the ones who are most able to empathize with people from all different walks of life. Emotions are the *same* in all human beings. And by the way, deep empathetic connections and emotional understanding transcends all the other cultural differences between people.

"Daniel Goleman, PhD, in his ground breaking book, *Emotional Intelligence,* analyzed 181 jobs in 121 organizations and found that emotional competencies were the best differentiators between star performers and typical performers. Emotions have the potential to get in the way of business relationships...and those who recognize the wounds and effect of their unhealed emotional "baggage" will no doubt make the most effective leaders. Daniel Goleman claims that Emotional

Intelligence is two times more important in contributing to excellence than intellect and expertise alone!

"Emotional Intelligence, to reiterate, is the ability to evaluate and manage your own emotions, and the emotions of the people around you.

"As adults, we have all developed elaborate defense mechanisms (in an attempt to block the pain from the unmet needs of our childhood). Strong leaders are in touch with their own feelings; and they have resolved most of their past negative emotional patterns within themselves. When the present moment is being interrupted by a past and painful memory, effective leaders know they are being "emotionally triggered" or a "button is being pushed" and they have a *choice* about how they *respond*. But most importantly, they resist the urge to *react* in a defensive manner.

"Compelling leaders embrace their own emotional challenges as the raw material required to reach their highest potential. They see challenging people and experiences as an opportunity for more emotional growth. So, in every moment, we have the opportunity to *detach* and *observe* and respond to life as it is unfolding right now, in the present moment.

Susan imagined herself standing Zen-like on a pedestal. People were throwing challenges at her, and she was calmly catching what was hers and deflecting what was not, back to her delegates. This image made her feel extremely empowered, centered and in control.

"Often in a moment of conflict we can *react* unconsciously through interpretations and beliefs based on our past painful experiences. When you are in a state of unconscious reaction, you are not fully present. When you react from your "blind spots," your can be certain that your own thinking is working against you.

"When we are caught up in our emotions, we do not see that those emotions are really coming from our own *thoughts* about the situation, versus the actual situation, itself. It's like looking through eyeglasses with a scratch on the lens; and thinking the same scratch that we are seeing over and over again in life, is actual reality.

So how do you identify a blind spot situation? Well, if the same types of dramas are happening to you, over and over again, this is a good indicator.

I have an exercise for you to help you identify these blind spots. It's in my eLearning program, but it is simple enough for you to do now. I'd like you to think of a past situation involving sadness or anger with your boss, or with someone who reports directly to you at work. I'd like you to notice how that thought makes you *feel* in the present moment.

Were you in charge of your emotions or were your emotions in charge of you? How did you respond in that situation? How could a different emotional response change the outcome of the conflict?

If you are experiencing a strong emotional reaction just thinking about this past situation, there is likely a blind spot there that needs to be explored.

Susan thought about how badly she wanted to hide and cry when she lost the Brown account. *Rejection*, she thought. *I felt personally rejected.* The thought made Susan sad, but she tried to follow the instructions and explore the source of that fear. Frankly, she was a middle child and most of her painful life circumstances had some form of perceived rejection or neglect...was that her 'scratched lens' that Ellen had been referring to?

As the call wrapped up, Susan started jotting down some negative thoughts and memories from childhood, determined to re-examine them as an adult.

Chapter Eight

Element #7: Maintain Presence

peak of the devil, Susan thought as she retrieved the battered envelope from her Inbox. Her recently lost clients—the Browns, had returned their Personal Impact Survey. It had been so long, she had given up on receiving a response. The envelope sat unopened on her desk an hour later. Susan had lost herself in crafting her sound bites and testimonials. Finally, she looked down in satisfaction at the testimonial pieced together from the first survey she had received back.

Susan is a fabulous Financial Planner and I highly recommend her! She helped us save money, get out of debt and overcome our self-defeating financial behaviors. Her customized and very detailed financial plan helped to lessen how overwhelmed we felt financially and was a great stress-relief.

Feeling bolstered by these good comments, she finally felt confident enough to open the Brown's envelope.

1. How did you come to work with Susan?

   Susan was assigned to us when our previous financial advisor retired.

2. What was your overall impression of Susan and her work?

   Overall, Susan was very kind and friendly to us.

3. What were the major benefits you received from working with Susan?

   She kept us from leaving the market in the economic downturn. That foresight saved us from postponing our retirement.

4. How could Susan have improved her work product and your experience of working with her?

    Although her advice was good, Susan sometimes didn't act like she believed in it. I always wondered if she was invested in what she was recommending for us. We ended up changing to another advisor we felt more confident about—one with more industry experience. I liked Susan a lot, but we just feel more secure with our new advisor.

5. How would you describe your experience with Susan to someone else in need of these services?

    Susan is smart and friendly and withheld any judgment when fielding our questions. She has a lot of patience and would be perfect for a young couple just starting out.

6. What three adjectives would you use to describe Susan?

    Smart, Sweet, Friendly

Susan couldn't figure out if she was happy or sad. The survey had said what a lot of others had concluded, that she was friendly, but didn't make them feel confident and secure in their investments. She was happy that she wasn't blindsided by a previously unknown fault, but sad that even though her advice was good, she had lost the Browns as clients anyway.

In the end, Susan decided that she was grateful. It hadn't been easy to send the survey; and she suspected that it had not been easy for the Browns to fill it out and return it, either. Although they had left her, they had cared enough to help with her personal and professional development. Susan pulled out a thank you note and began to put her gratitude on paper.

Once the thank you note was out in the mail, Susan reflected, *I didn't cry. I didn't even feel the urge.* She paused for a moment to enjoy the feeling of pride at this significant personal accomplishment.

* * *

Sanjay gritted his teeth as he left the meeting. It had been terrible, a complete fiasco. He had listened. He had acknowledged. He had done everything he had been taught to do. And it had all gone wrong.

"Sanjay!" David called out to him.

Sanjay was tempted to pretend he didn't hear him, but he reminded himself that David had been his biggest ally the last few weeks. He slowed down for David to catch up.

"You okay? I could tell you were taking a beating in there."

"It was rough," Sanjay conceded.

They walked in silence for a moment. Sanjay wasn't entirely sure where he was going, but David didn't seem too troubled by this. He seemed lost in thought himself.

David finally spoke up, "Did you ever see that Mel Gibson movie where he can read women's thoughts?"

Sanjay nodded. Susan had made him sit through a re-run on cable.

"Even though he knows what they are thinking, at first he still says everything wrong."

Sanjay thought he knew where this was going. "Was that me in there?"

David nodded.

"I think I should give up on this whole empathy business and go back to being myself," he sighed.

"Nope," David countered. "You are going to keep working on it. Practice makes perfect."

"Practice might get me fired," Sanjay replied dryly.

David laughed. "We're all replaceable, sure. This isn't about work, this is about you and your self-growth." When Sanjay didn't say anything,

David asked, "How are things at home?"

Despite his mood, Sanjay smiled. "Things are going really well," he admitted.

"Keep working on it," David smiled and patted Sanjay on the shoulder before heading in the direction of his own cubicle.

"I will," Sanjay agreed, long after David was gone.

* * *

David gestured to a seat next to him at the conference table when the team met for the personal branding call an hour later. Sanjay smiled and accepted the invitation. He had always liked David, but he suspected that they might become actual friends. It would be a nice change.

"I'm going to start off today's webinar a little differently." Ellen burst onto the line. There is a quote I'd like to share with you that perfectly fits today's very important subject. Walt Whitman said, *"We convince by our presence."* And today's Element is Element Seven: Maintain Presence.

"Influential leaders show up for life living in the moment and fully present. Presence is a state of *being*, versus something that you *do*. It's about living in the here and now—without obsessing about the future, or dwelling in the past. It's about really *being* with yourself and other people, without the distractions of a busy, worrying, or critical mind. It's about stopping to really see, appreciate and smell the roses."

Wow, Ellen is sure passionate about this Element. We are getting right to the point today! Sanjay thought.

"Being present is not about feeling good or bad, but rather, it's about feeling everything, in a much more sensitive, non-judgmental and centered way. Fully present people see, hear and experience more. Effective leaders have presence because they have cultivated and expanded awareness of their own emotions and those of others around them. This opens them up to having more authentic relationships, because when you are fully present and have quieted your own mind chatter, you *feel* and *observe* more of the world around you. And it becomes much easier to connect authentically with others.

"We give our thoughts meaning—but as we discussed last week, it's just made up meaning, seen through our own "scratched" and distorted lens. It's often far from the truth of what's really going on. But please do not forget about Element #1 and about the importance of Consciously Managing Your State of Mind. Because, the way you internally think about yourself and your circumstances creates an energy force around you, which is felt by people and subconsciously impacts and influences them.

"In the present, our emotions feel like the reality of the moment. If you're focused on the past or on negative circumstances that have held you back, you will project negative feelings and create a negative reality. And this projection will repel positive opportunities.

Am I generating my own negativity? Sanjay wondered.

"We generate our personal reality in our heads, and people use thoughts very differently. Everyone is making up what they see, moment to moment, based on their own separate realities. Fear, insecurity and self-doubt are merely symptoms of our state of mind. The good news is that confidence, security, peacefulness and happiness are also symptoms of our state of mind. It's up to you to choose.

"According to Michael Brown, Author of *The Presence Process,* Present Moment Awareness is: when you are physically present, mentally clear, emotionally balanced and spiritually connected. To the extent that you are fully present, you're able to take in your experiences on many levels. This observing part of you allows you to observe and let go of the habitual knee-jerk reactions of your personality, that have kept you trapped for so long.

"There are three major states of mind that keep us from being present and in the moment:

1. Busy Mind

2. Worrying Mind

3. Critical Mind

Typically, we are more inclined to one particular style of not being present.

"One of the ways people are not fully present is when they are distracted by their own busy mind. People afflicted with their own non-stop mind chatter, find that their awareness is so completely taken up with their perpetual inner dialogue of distraction, racing from one thought to the next, that they do not experience themselves as separate from that dialog. If you have a busy mind that's difficult to turn off, you're not completely present with the person you are sitting across from.

"Then there's the second reason people are not fully present...and they are the worriers of the world. People who worry are usually focused on precisely the things they *don't* want to happen. They can't be present in the moment because they are fearful of the future. The anxiety and negative thoughts that accompany a worrying mind tends to attract those very same things that they're worrying about! This becomes a never-ending, self-fulfilling cycle of negativity.

"The third pre-disposition to not being present is having a critical mind, where your mind judges everything. It compares one thing or person or experience to another. This sort of thinking keeps us stuck in the past and drowning in our own limited judgments about the way we think things are, versus the way they really are."

Yep, Sanjay thought. *I have a critical mind. I'm always thinking about if something is true or not. I'm always skipping ahead in conversations, especially if I think they don't know what they are talking about.*

"I hope you registered which one of these three you predominantly are, because having one or more of these distracted mind states can lead to serious health problems. You busy-minded people who are distracted all the time. You may be nodding like you're listening. Or maybe you're doing five different things at once and barely listening at all. You're the Type A personalities, and you're more likely to die of a heart attack than the rest of us. There is a link between circulation issues and having a busy-mind.

"When you're worrying-minded, you're one of those people like my own mother. My mom gets a cold and it seems to never go away. Instead, it settles down into her respiratory tract, and she winds up with bronchitis for two months. Worrying-minded people tend to have respiratory problems.

"Critical-minded people, unfortunately, are prone to an *emotional* issue, rather than a physical one. It's called depression. Since critical-minded people are usually perfectionists they are never truly happy, because we live in a very imperfect world. So critical-minded people tend to be disappointed a lot and therefore they suffer from depression more than the rest of the population.

I bet Susan is a busy-minded person. I'll have to ask her, Sanjay noted.

"I'd like you to take a minute right now, and ask yourselves which one of these ways of being are you predominantly demonstrating at work? Are you mostly busy-minded and distracted? Are you mostly worrying? Or, are you mostly critical-minded and running constant critical commentary on everything and everyone?"

Critical.

"The way people perceive you at work, has everything to do with your ability to influence. By getting fully present, your energetic influence will make people feel seen and heard in a way that erases all thoughts of doubt and uncertainty and creates instant trust and rapport. When you are quiet, calm and present in your body, you become most attractive to others and can more easily influence them. That's because when you quiet your thinking, people can actually *feel* you and the presence of your innate wisdom, just *being* with them in the present moment... and that's irresistible! When you're present, you gain access to higher mental states, like intuition; and you feel like you're "in the flow" and good things start happening effortlessly.

"There are six practices for becoming more present in my eLearning program, but we are going to go over them here, as well. First, create an intention to get present before you engage with someone. It is only by consciously making the decision to be present that you can actually become more present."

I can do that, Sanjay thought, relieved that it could be so easy.

"Second, commit to avoid any multi-tasking when you are in someone else's presence. Turn off all electronic devices and pay full attention. Your brain can only do one thing at a time, despite what our culture, family, and work colleagues think that you should be able to juggle. Multi-tasking doesn't work, so stop trying!

"Third, mentally note when you find yourself distracted. Catch yourself whenever you're busy, worrying or your critical mind derails your concentration.

"Fourth, when you catch yourself "leaving the scene" mentally, imagine there is a door you can close and leave behind whatever is distracting you. After mentally "closing the door," refocus your full attention on your breathing and on the person you are with.

Fifth, choose to approach others with compassion, and leave all of your judgments behind. Remember that everyone has something to offer. This will help you suspend judgment and search for that unique attribute of the person you are interacting with.

Okay, I'm going to have to concentrate on that one, Sanjay noted.

Finally, when you start to make assumptions, stop and ask yourself: Do I know what the reality really is? Or do I need to check my assumptions and the meaning I am making up about it? Remember, we all view the world through a distorted lens. Be willing to conduct a reality check every once in awhile.

"Ellen," a voice interrupted. "I find sometimes, especially when it's a topic I'm not particularly interested in—my mind can easily wander away. When I'm not interested I get distracted by my phone."

"I hate to tell you this, but as I just said a little while ago, it is time to put away the phone." Ellen said bluntly. "It is an easy out from the current moment. Being present is about living in the here and now without obsessing about the future or dwelling in the past. It's about really being with yourself and other people without distractions. It's about stopping to see and smell the flowers. Being present isn't about feeling good or bad. It's about taking it all in. It's about feeling everything in a much more sensitive, non-judgmental, and centered way. Once you put your phone and any other distractions away, you will broaden your opportunity to fully interact and appreciate the world around you."

Sanjay felt his phone buzz in his pocket. He smiled to himself at the irony of pulling out his phone in this room, at this moment. He resolved to wait until the conference call wrapped up.

The webinar wrapped up quickly and it wasn't too long before he stepped out of the conference room. Curious, he pulled out his phone.

"Less phones around the kids! We need to be fully present with them, too!"

If there was a guilty party to staring at phones in front of the kids, it was Susan, not Sanjay. He spent all day interacting with technology. It was a relief to play with the kids when he got home. He smiled at her text and replied, "Deal!"

Chapter Nine

Element #8: Authentically Project Your True Self

Susan sprawled on the couch, completely wiped out. The kids were in bed and the TV was off. It was nice to have a moment of quiet to just think! Sanjay must have felt the same way too. He came into the living room holding two glasses of wine, handed her one and then proceeded to settle himself on the couch with her feet in his lap.

"It's been a wild couple of weeks," Sanjay offered after a few moments of silence.

It was such an understatement that Susan began to chuckle and then to outright laugh. Pretty soon Sanjay joined in too and they were both laughing like mad loons on the couch.

When the laughter ran its course and Susan caught her breath and wiped the tears from her eyes, she realized how good she felt. "We are so lucky, you know?"

Sanjay nodded. "I don't think I've told you the half of it."

"Really?" she asked, genuinely curious. "How so?"

"Well I know we both talked about the Personal Impact Surveys, but there's been so much more to these *Eight Elements*. I feel like every week I learn a little bit more about myself; and now I have these profound insights into not only work stuff, but life stuff, too. Like when I was a kid, I was teased mercilessly in grade school. I really started building walls then. I thought that I would be a whole new person when I went to University in London, but I was so out of place! I just retreated more."

"I can see that," Susan allowed, "but you've never been like that with me. That first time we met in the cafeteria, you couldn't stop talking!"

"A beautiful woman was paying attention to me," Sanjay grinned. "And we had London in common. I would be a fool to let that moment pass me by."

Susan grinned broadly. "You are many things, but never a fool."

Sanjay gave her foot a squeeze. "What about you? What have you learned?"

"Well on the work side, I've definitely been self-sabotaging my meetings. I've been so busy trying to build rapport and make friends that I haven't projected confidence in my own financial advising ability."

"Seriously?" Sanjay was truly floored. "You are one of the most confident people I know."

"Yeah. I had this folksy persona going on. It was great for getting appointments, but when it came time to close, it was working against me and my professionalism."

Susan smiled as Sanjay gave her a sideways 'you're crazy' glance. "Fine! Don't believe me," she playfully smacked his arm. "Your turn. What else have you learned?"

Sanjay nodded to himself. "Did you know, that people like to feel like they've been heard? It's like they don't like to be talked over and contradicted."

Susan opened her eyes wide in mock shock, "I can't imagine how that could be!"

"Yes! I know!" Sanjay took her teasing well. "It's like they have feelings that need to be acknowledged. It's so strange."

"Speaking of strange," Susan volunteered. "I had a realization that my humble husband may not take credit for what he does because it is a cultural no-no where he is from." Susan held her breath. She hoped she hadn't pushed the conversation too far.

Sanjay looked far away, but gave her foot another reassuring squeeze. "You Americans brag too much."

Susan took that as a sign that it was okay to push a little further. "My husband is brilliant and wise, and deserves to be acknowledged for his individual contributions."

"I'm working on it," he smiled and then proceeded to regale her with the story of value that he and David had worked on together. When he finished, she clapped enthusiastically.

"Your turn," Sanjay prompted. She could tell by the flush in his cheeks that he was a little embarrassed by her applause. She knew what she wanted to talk about, and it seemed like it was finally the right moment.

"I think that I struggle with super-human versus extra-human," she confessed. "It's not easy to juggle work, family, friends...a life. As my business gets bigger, I worry how I'm going to manage it all. To be there for you, the kids, my clients, and be able to maintain myself and my own sanity. It seems like too much for any one person to manage." She sounded like she was complaining about success. Susan fought the urge to cry and scold herself.

"You could make a million dollars a year, but if you weren't here for the kids, and me, it wouldn't be worth it," he said softly. "I know I've pushed you to make more money. But this whole personal branding thing...it has a way of changing priorities."

Susan felt a wave a relief sweep over her body. She wasn't sure what she had been afraid of, but his response was perfect. "You've really gotten good at the empathy thing." She smiled.

"Come here," he opened his arms to her.

"I love you."

"I love you, too."

* * *

Sanjay was surprised how excited he was for the last of the personal branding webinars. Ever since he and Susan had sat down for their heart-to-heart, things had just felt like they were coming together. Projects at work were going smoothly, Marty had good things to say about Sanjay's contribution to the team. Susan was more present in their home life, and he could tell that he was getting better at actively listening in the present moment and empathizing with her.

The conference room was buzzing with an excited energy today. He wasn't the only one feeling a difference, now that the personal branding program was coming to an end. Everyone was smiling and making eye contact. What a difference, Sanjay thought, from that first session, where people barely interacted with one another, much less made eye contact and smiled at one another! Soon the hold music was replaced with Ellen's voice, welcoming them to the last session of the webinar series.

"Today we are going to take a moment to reflect on the past eight weeks. I'll answer a few questions and please feel free to share any thoughts you might have. Then, we are going to explore masks and the roles that we play in our day-to-day lives that keep us from living authentically.

A few people volunteered their experiences and how things had changed for the better in the last few weeks. "Hi Ellen, this is Greta in London. I'm still having trouble on an earlier Element. I think it's my people skills?" Greta didn't seem too sure of herself. "I would definitely like to be seen more as an influencer. I looked back at some of the adjectives I received from the surveys and found that one of the things that came across repeatedly was 'informative, but sometimes too candid and direct.' Sometimes being too direct and too candid can hinder your ability to influence. It's something that I'm working on, but I recognize that I struggle with that."

"That's great self-awareness." Ellen replied. "One of the ways to combat this sort of perception is to concentrate on building warmth and empathy, and that will soften your directness and candor; and people will open up to you more.

"And I just want to remind you that the ability to project your true self increases the trust and rapport that you build with other people. Wearing a mask to protect your true self actually destroys the perception of self-confidence and your ability to influence others. That brings us to today's final Element Eight: Authentically Project Your True Self. We do this by taking off the mask we've created as a defense.

"Energetic influencers can authentically connect with and inspire others because they have successfully completed their own emotional work. They no longer need to hide behind a mask, pretending to be some idealized version of themself. It's about your willingness and preparedness to expose your true feelings, vulnerabilities, and thoughts. Being able to express your vulnerability is what makes you more emotionally intelligent and much more likeable and approachable.

"The mask develops from thinking that you are not enough just as you are...it comes from a lack of self-acceptance and a lack of self-appreciation. When you are in your masked self, you are focused on protecting yourself, and thus cut off from your own inner source of authentic power. Created in reaction to past pain and rejection, the false self or mask is designed to try to please, fend off, and control others."

I definitely try to fend people off with my mask, Sanjay admitted to himself. *My mask is designed to avoid uncomfortable situations. And I avoid confrontation at any cost, both at work and at home.*

"Most people have tried to protect themselves and control their lives by putting on a false self or a "mask" between the outside world and their inner vulnerability. We think it protects us from getting hurt (the way we were hurt or rejected as children, most likely due to the "imperfect" parenting most of us received); but all it really does is cut us off from our own inner source of real power. The authentic self-expression of our true self, alone and out there and undefended can be a terrifying idea for many adults.

"Until the adult re-experiences and releases the original childhood hurts (preferably with a trained professional therapist), these painful wounds remain frozen in the personality and continue to be re-enacted in our present-day reality."

I wonder if I can spare my kids some of this grief, Sanjay thought. *What would it take for them to live authentically their entire lives?*

"The danger of living with a false self or a mask, is that you can always be triggered when your self-esteem feels threatened. Think of the last time you received a critical remark, a cool reception, or an opposing opinion. These things can expose us and make us vulnerable to buried pain from the past.

"Having a mask that you think you need to constantly defend your own value and acceptability, creates the constant fear of being inadequate (or just not "perfect" enough)...and it certainly obliterates any feeling of confidence (yours in yourself or others' in you). And remember, confidence is the #1 reason people buy or choose anything. If we live a life expecting rejection or disapproval from being ourselves, we will continue to attract people that confirm our worst fears about ourselves.

"Being willing and prepared to remove your mask and expose your true feelings, vulnerabilities and thoughts makes you a much more influential leader. True vulnerability comes from having the power of not needing protection, because there's nothing to defend or react to anymore."

Sanjay took a moment to let that sink in. Vulnerability and power did not seem like they would go hand-in-hand, but the way Ellen had explained it, he could see the connection. The man who is covered in armor, may be protected, but he is always expecting to be attacked. The man who walks with a sense of inner confidence, with nothing to hide or defend, doesn't need any protection. Sanjay made a few notes to think about in the future.

As our personal branding webinar program comes to a close, I'd like to take a moment to reiterate the *Eight Elements.* They are:

Consciously Manage Your State of Mind

Have Self-Awareness

Artfully Communicate

Radiate Likeability and Empathy

Inspire Confidence

Serve as a Leader

Maintain Presence

Authentically Project Your True Self

"Additionally, the first letter of these *Eight Elements,* when combined, spell the word *Charisma.* Charisma is that rare combination of warmth and strength and keeping them equally balanced has everything to do with your ability to influence.

"Each of the *Eight Elements* inter-relate. They work together as an interwoven web of inner attributes that make up your personal brand. As you learn to incorporate all of the *Eight Elements* into everything you do, you will naturally enhance your confidence, presence, and influence and become a more compelling leader.

"The last activity that I will ask you to do is to repeat taking the *Influence Inquiry* from the beginning of the webinar series. The *Influence Inquiry* really helps you understand which of the *Eight Elements* might need a little more development for you."

Sanjay grinned to himself. His first scores had been dismal. He looked forward to seeing his results this time.

"So notice on your own *Influence Inquiry,* any low scores that seem glaring to you; because those are the areas that I believe you could review and bolster up, just by understanding the qualities and skills to develop. And yes, you can learn energetic influence, because it's an inside job.

"When you really 'get' all *Eight Elements* internally, they just radiate externally and make you irresistible as a person and a personal brand.

When the seminar ended and Ellen signed off, everyone stayed around the conference table wrapped up in their own thoughts. Finally, Sanjay cleared his throat.

"I know this is a bit out of the blue, but I would just like to say that I really liked this program. I learned a lot about myself that I didn't expect. Some of it was hard, and some of it I just made hard for myself. Ultimately though, I'd like you to all know that this is something I intend to keep working on, past these eight weeks. I really feel like it has been valuable for my professional and personal growth, and I look forward to growing within our team, as well."

Sanjay blushed. He hadn't meant to give a speech. But he had meant it. A quick glance down the table made him realize that his testimonial was very well received. People were smiling and Marty was nodding in approval. Sanjay felt like things were only going to go up from here.

Epilogue

Six Months Later

"Four bedrooms!" Sanjay announced as he hopped back in the car.

"Not a bad neighborhood either," Susan noted. "What's the asking price?"

Sanjay consulted the flyer he had picked up. "It's in our budget."

Susan couldn't believe how quickly their lives were changing. Just six months ago, this house search would have been fraught with tension and unsaid anxieties. She had been managing her state of mind, refusing to let her many misgivings turn passive aggressive. Sanjay had been amazingly open and receptive when she needed to talk through what she was feeling.

The phone was ringing through the Bluetooth connection in the car. Susan could see it was her assistant.

"Hi Mary, what's up?"

Mary had been a great find. Not only did she connect with Susan, but she knew her job and really made Susan's clients feel comfortable.

"You won't believe who just called!" Mary's enthusiasm was bubbling through the phone.

"Tell me!"

"John and Sarah! They want to move ahead with you!"

Susan felt her jaw drop. Sanjay quietly offered his hand in a high five. She had kept in contact with John and Sarah through a monthly newsletter and happened to bump into them at a barbeque the previous week. Apparently her confident new attitude and her more grounded demeanor had paid off!

"That's amazing! That's..."

"Three new clients this month, I know! The paperwork is out in the mail already, I just knew you would be excited."

"I am! Thanks for calling!"

Sanjay took her hand and kissed it. "I'm so proud of you!"

Just then, a voice piped up from the back seat, "Does this mean we're rich?"

Susan and Sanjay both laughed and turned to their attention to the backseat where Josh and Lily were strapped in.

"Well not exactly, but we're getting there! Mommy just got a new client." Sanjay started.

"And Daddy got a big promotion at work," Susan finished.

Sanjay had come home with champagne and flowers three months ago. He was now lead engineer of the Innovation Lab and truly thriving in his new position. When she asked, he gave all the credit to Element Four, and his newly-discovered ability to "Radiate Likeability and Empathy" with ease and confidence. It made her chuckle because he was still so humble and introverted, but she had to admit, he had worked hard on his empathy and his leadership skills.

Susan reflected on how deeply she loved Sanjay, how easy he was to love. *We are living life in a whole new league now,* Susan marveled. Personally, professionally, their life just had so much new depth; and she was excited to continue the exploration.

Sanjay warmly touched Susan's 'baby bump' thinking they should tell the kids about their soon-to-be-born, new sibling; but the car just wasn't the right place. They drove to the park so the kids could play and they could both get fully present before they shared the big news.

Neither Susan nor Sanjay had any idea what the kids' reactions to a new brother or sister might be, but she wanted the moment they learned about it, to be very special for all of them.

"Go play!" Susan shouted as her children made a beeline for the playground.

Sanjay quietly came up behind her and wrapped his arms around her. She leaned into him and he into her—together they were stronger than ever and their future never looked brighter.

Appendix

———

Pre-*Influence Inquiry*

Personal Impact Survey

Cover Letter and Instructions

Adjective Box Debrief

Testimonial Worksheet

Ten Tips for Connecting Emotionally

Post-*Influence Inquiry*

The Pre-*Influence Inquiry*

Given the benefits, your "Energetic Presence" has to enhance your personal brand and your influence on others, it's important to learn how influential you currently are. *The Influence Inquiry* will help you access your personal strengths and identify areas for developing greater influence.

For each statement below, click the appropriate box to indicate how closely it represents the "true you" on an average day. Try not to over-think your answers. Just be candid and completely honest with yourself.

Element 1: Consciously Manage Your State of Mind

	Never True				Always True	
	1	2	3	4	5	6
1. I am aware of my innermost thoughts.	☐	☐	☐	☐	☐	☐
2. I can quickly turn around my negative thinking.	☐	☐	☐	☐	☐	☐
3. I focus on the positive experiences that have helped me grow.	☐	☐	☐	☐	☐	☐
4. I trust my intuitive wisdom.	☐	☐	☐	☐	☐	☐

Element 2: Have Self-Awareness

	Never True				Always True	
	1	2	3	4	5	6
5. I recognize how my feelings affect my performance.	☐	☐	☐	☐	☐	☐
6. I make others feel comfortable around me.	☐	☐	☐	☐	☐	☐
7. I am aware of my impact on others.	☐	☐	☐	☐	☐	☐
8. My verbal messages match my non-verbal messages.	☐	☐	☐	☐	☐	☐

Element 3: Artfully Communicate

	Never True			Always True		
	1	2	3	4	5	6
9. I quickly build meaningful rapport with others.	☐	☐	☐	☐	☐	☐
10. I engage others with thought-provoking questions.	☐	☐	☐	☐	☐	☐
11. I tell compelling stories that illustrate my value.	☐	☐	☐	☐	☐	☐
12. I intentionally listen to others without having pre-set expectations.	☐	☐	☐	☐	☐	☐

Element 4: Radiate Likeability and Empathy

	Never True			Always True		
	1	2	3	4	5	6
13. Others consider me to be a friendly person.	☐	☐	☐	☐	☐	☐
14. I appreciate others for who they are.	☐	☐	☐	☐	☐	☐
15. I am curious about other people's life experiences.	☐	☐	☐	☐	☐	☐
16. I take an active interest in the concerns of others.	☐	☐	☐	☐	☐	☐

Element 5: Inspire Confidence

	Never True			Always True		
	1	2	3	4	5	6
17. My beliefs support me in what I want to accomplish.	☐	☐	☐	☐	☐	☐
18. I am sure of my own capabilities.	☐	☐	☐	☐	☐	☐
19. When I experience self-doubt, I manage my own thinking.	☐	☐	☐	☐	☐	☐
20. When I feel insecure, I am able to reassure myself.	☐	☐	☐	☐	☐	☐

Element 6: Serve as a Leader

	Never True			Always True		
	1	2	3	4	5	6
21. People are naturally attracted to me.	☐	☐	☐	☐	☐	☐
22. I can see possibilities where others do not.	☐	☐	☐	☐	☐	☐
23. I am able to inspire others to support my cause.	☐	☐	☐	☐	☐	☐
24. I manage my own emotional responses.	☐	☐	☐	☐	☐	☐

Element 7: Maintain Presence

	Never True			Always True		
	1	2	3	4	5	6
25. I bring my "whole self" to interactions with others.	☐	☐	☐	☐	☐	☐
26. I restrain my wandering mind during interactions.	☐	☐	☐	☐	☐	☐
27. I focus on what's happening in the moment.	☐	☐	☐	☐	☐	☐
28. I am able to make others feel seen.	☐	☐	☐	☐	☐	☐

Element 8: Authentically Project Your True Self

	Never True			Always True		
	1	2	3	4	5	6
29. I expose my true feelings.	☐	☐	☐	☐	☐	☐
30. I know what energizes me.	☐	☐	☐	☐	☐	☐
31. I know what depletes my energy.	☐	☐	☐	☐	☐	☐
32. I act in alignment with my values.	☐	☐	☐	☐	☐	☐

Personal Impact Survey

1. How did you come to work with [*insert your name*]?

2. What was your overall impression of [*insert your name*] and their work?

3. What were the major benefits you received from working with [*insert your name*]?

4. How could [*insert your name*] have improved their work product and your experience of working with him/her?

5. How would you describe your experience with [*insert your name*] to someone else in need of these services?

6. What three adjectives would you use to describe [*insert your name*]?

Cover Letter

Date

From: Address

To: Address

Dear [personalize with their name]:

As a highly valued colleague/client, your feedback means a lot to me personally and to the growth of my career/business.

I am working on a personal branding project to help me improve and expand my professional opportunities. As part of the process, I have selected 5 colleagues/clients to give me some feedback about me and my work.

I was wondering if you would be so kind as to take a few minutes and complete the attached *Personal Impact Survey.*

Thanks in advance for your much appreciated candid feedback.

Warmest regards,

P.S. I would appreciate your responses no later than [give a 2 week window for the actual deadline for a reply]

Fifteen Adjectives

Record the adjectives from your clients and colleagues in the table below.

Person 1	Person 2	Person 3	Person 4	Person 5

Testimonials Worksheet

Once you've received approval for the re-worked testimonials, record them in the table below.

Name & Title	Approved Testimonial(s)

Ten Tips for Connecting Emotionally:

1. Smile a big, warm smile (early and often).

2. Develop a sense of humor.

3. Notice the color of a person's eyes and remember names and details.

4. Exude positive energy, confidence and empathy.

5. Give sincere compliments.

6. When you're feeling emotionally triggered, breathe deeply a few times before responding .

7. Respond more to energy and emotions than to words.

8. Maintain an authentic interest in life and people.

9. Become as conscious of the world around you as you are of yourself.

10. Quiet your mind to become more present and sensitive in the moment.

The Post-*Influence Inquiry*

Now that you have completed your learning of the *Eight Elements of Influence*, it is time to check in with your personal growth. Take this inquiry for the second time, to gage your personal brand and your influence on others. When you have completed the *Influence Inquiry*, compare it to the pre-course inquiry to access your personal growth and identify areas for further development of influence.

For each statement below, click the appropriate box to indicate how closely it represents the "true you" on an average day. Try not to over-think your answers. Just be candid and completely honest with yourself.

Element 1: Consciously Manage Your State of Mind

	Never True			Always True		
	1	2	3	4	5	6
1. I am aware of my innermost thoughts.	☐	☐	☐	☐	☐	☐
2. I can quickly turn around my negative thinking.	☐	☐	☐	☐	☐	☐
3. I focus on the positive experiences that have helped me grow.	☐	☐	☐	☐	☐	☐
4. I trust my intuitive wisdom.	☐	☐	☐	☐	☐	☐

Element 2: Have Self-Awareness

	Never True			Always True		
	1	2	3	4	5	6
5. I recognize how my feelings affect my performance.	☐	☐	☐	☐	☐	☐
6. I make others feel comfortable around me.	☐	☐	☐	☐	☐	☐
7. I am aware of my impact on others.	☐	☐	☐	☐	☐	☐
8. My verbal messages match my non-verbal messages.	☐	☐	☐	☐	☐	☐

Element 3: Artfully Communicate

	Never True			Always True		
	1	2	3	4	5	6
9. I quickly build meaningful rapport with others.	☐	☐	☐	☐	☐	☐
10. I engage others with thought-provoking questions.	☐	☐	☐	☐	☐	☐
11. I tell compelling stories that illustrate my value.	☐	☐	☐	☐	☐	☐
12. I intentionally listen to others without having pre-set expectations.	☐	☐	☐	☐	☐	☐

Element 4: Radiate Likeability and Empathy

	Never True			Always True		
	1	2	3	4	5	6
13. Others consider me to be a friendly person.	☐	☐	☐	☐	☐	☐
14. I appreciate others for who they are.	☐	☐	☐	☐	☐	☐
15. I am curious about other people's life experiences.	☐	☐	☐	☐	☐	☐
16. I take an active interest in the concerns of others.	☐	☐	☐	☐	☐	☐

Element 5: Inspire Confidence

	Never True			Always True		
	1	2	3	4	5	6
17. My beliefs support me in what I want to accomplish.	☐	☐	☐	☐	☐	☐
18. I am sure of my own capabilities.	☐	☐	☐	☐	☐	☐
19. When I experience self-doubt, I manage my own thinking.	☐	☐	☐	☐	☐	☐
20. When I feel insecure, I am able to reassure myself.	☐	☐	☐	☐	☐	☐

Element 6: Serve as a Leader

	Never True			Always True		
	1	2	3	4	5	6
21. People are naturally attracted to me.	☐	☐	☐	☐	☐	☐
22. I can see possibilities where others do not.	☐	☐	☐	☐	☐	☐
23. I am able to inspire others to support my cause.	☐	☐	☐	☐	☐	☐
24. I manage my own emotional responses.	☐	☐	☐	☐	☐	☐

Element 7: Maintain Presence

	Never True			Always True		
	1	2	3	4	5	6
25. I bring my "whole self" to interactions with others.	☐	☐	☐	☐	☐	☐
26. I restrain my wandering mind during interactions.	☐	☐	☐	☐	☐	☐
27. I focus on what's happening in the moment.	☐	☐	☐	☐	☐	☐
28. I am able to make others feel seen.	☐	☐	☐	☐	☐	☐

Element 8: Authentically Project Your True Self

	Never True			Always True		
	1	2	3	4	5	6
29. I expose my true feelings.	☐	☐	☐	☐	☐	☐
30. I know what energizes me.	☐	☐	☐	☐	☐	☐
31. I know what depletes my energy.	☐	☐	☐	☐	☐	☐
32. I act in alignment with my values.	☐	☐	☐	☐	☐	☐

Next Steps

For more information, re: scheduling an Interactive Keynote Talk, a live, full day "Thought Leadership" training, global webinars, private personal brand and influence-building coaching and business branding, please contact Ellen Looyen directly at:

ellen@ellen4branding.com

PH: 925.284.5828 (PST)

To purchase Ellen's comprehensive, 2-module, brand and influence-building eLearning program for yourself or for your work team:

www.ellen4branding.com

Ellen's Suggested Supplemental Reading List

The Soul of Money...By: Lynne Twist

Compelling People...By: Jeff Neffinger and Matthew Kohut

The Presence Process... By: Michael Brown

Emotional Intelligence...By: Daniel Goleman

The Power of Now...By: Eckhart Tolle

CPSIA information can be obtained
at www.ICGtesting.com
Printed in the USA
FSOW02n0210030516
19883FS